AF413123

THICKER THAN WATER

Gregory Lamont Hemphill

Thicker than water

Published by Spines

ISBN: 979-8-89383-204-4

THICKER THAN WATER

GREGORY LAMONT HEMPHILL

CONTENTS

CHAPTER ONE

"DAVID, get in here and eat this food," his mother shouted.

"Okay, Mommy!"

She was a single mother, trying her best to provide the bare necessities for her son. The loss of her husband was a blow, but she knew for the sake of her son, she needed to go on. Every time she looked in his eyes she saw Rudy. He was a handsome five-eleven, one hundred-eighty pounds, green eyes, curly hair, and bo-legged.

The two of them were in love with each other despite the fact that their parents didn't approve. Mainly because she was a beautiful black woman and he was white. She was a short, outspoken, brown-eyed, jet black hair, smooth brown skin, beautiful woman.

Every day she feared for her son's life and hers, knowing what she knew. The information was given to her by her husband that one horrific day on his deathbed. Hanging onto this secret was like holding onto a bomb.

Wiping mud on his clean clothes, "Momma, did you cook macaroni and cheese?" David asked.

"No, cheeseburgers and fries."

"Yay," he said, running to the bathroom to wash his hands.

She always followed him into the bathroom to make sure he

did. Sometimes he would put the soap between his hands and say they were clean. There were never any suds in the sink that were dirty, so that was a giveaway.

"Look young man, you wash your hands with soap and water or no dessert," she said, turning on the faucet.

"Momma, why do I have to always wash my hands?" he asked.

"Because when little boys don't wash their hands, they get sick and can't eat dessert."

She put her hands on his and started to wash their hands together. He looked up and smiled at her as she smiled back at him. Elaine grabbed his favorite towel off the towel rack and dried their hands. She gave him a horsey back ride into the kitchen.

Later on that night, David had eaten all this food and was ready for bed. She remembered buying his pajamas with his father on his birthday. After tucking him in, she kissed him goodnight and turned out the light.

Pretending he was sleeping, he opened his eyes, "I love you, Mommy, goodnight."

"I love you too, baby, goodnight."

She closed the door to his room and thought about the many nights his father and her would kiss him goodnight.

While locking up the house, Elaine noticed a car parked in the front of the house. She tried seeing who was inside the car, but it was too dark. What she did see was there were two men in the car. Paying it little mind, she walked upstairs to her bedroom and went to sleep.

The next morning, Elaine felt something crawling on her face and woke up to find it was David with his toy spider.

"Wake up, Mommy," he said smiling.

"Give Mommy five more minutes, ok?"

"Okay, time to wake up again, Mommy," he laughed.

Pulling the covers off of her, "What do you want Mommy to cook for you?" she asked.

"Pancakes, waffles, sausage, eggs, and–"

Interrupting him, "Wait a minute, Mommy can't cook all that. How about some pancakes and sausages?"

"Okay"

"Now go brush your teeth and wash your face," she said, giving him a kiss on his forehead.

The doorbell rang downstairs and Elaine went to answer it. She opened the door's curtain to see who it was. It was Mr. Simms, the mailman. He was always polite and had a smile on his face. He was also a flirt with all the ladies in the neighborhood.

"Hello and Good Morning, Mrs. Devant," he said grinning from ear to ear.

"Hello, Mr. Simms, and Good Morning to you."

"I'm sorry to hear about your husband," he said, trying to look into her house.

"May I help you with something?" she asked.

"I was just admiring how nice your home looks"

"May I have my mail please?" Elaine asked.

Handing her the mail, "I'm sorry, I didn't mean to be nosey."

"Goodbye, Mr. Simms," slamming the door in his face.

She locked the door and went upstairs to shower, so she could fix breakfast for her and David. Some time had passed, she came into the kitchen, and found everything ready for her. Elaine made breakfast and got the school bag ready for David.

She walked out the door with David and went to the corner to take him to his bus stop. While she was putting his jacket and hat on, she watched his grandparents driving up and parking across the street.

The two of them were getting out of the car and started walking towards her and David. Elaine looked over at them in disgust, for the lack of compassion for their loss.

Grabbing hold of her son, "What the hell do you two want?"

"We just came to talk and maybe see our grandson if that was okay?" his grandmother asked.

Elaine was never diplomatic when it came to her son's grandparents, but she decided to be for her son's sake. She moved him in front of her so they could see him.

"He's so adorable, he looks just like his father," his grandmother said. Elaine Looked at the two of them wondering what they were up to this time, She knew something was happening, but not sure what. She quickly moved David back behind her.

"The two of you are being so friendly, why is that?" she asked.

"We're just trying to get involved in his life and to help you, if you need it," his grandmother replied.

"Where was all this love when I was married to your son and he was alive?" Elaine asked,

"We were wrong."

"The world must be coming to an end," she said sarcastically.

"Please, Elaine, give us another chance, we've learned from our mistakes," David's grandfather said.

"I'll think about it."

The school bus came and she helped David onto the bus. She walked past his grandparents without saying a word and went home. The two of them looked on in shame, She knew she'd have to stand her ground or she would lose her son too.

CHAPTER
TWO

IT WAS ten o'clock and Elaine was at home cleaning up. She was at the kitchen sink washing dishes reminiscing about Rudy. He had a habit of spraying the window from the outside with the water hose. Tears rolled from her eyes down her smooth skin. This was a rough year for her and David, and it wasn't getting any better.

She finished the dishes and went into the sitting room, not far from the kitchen. She sat on the couch, staring out of the window into the backyard. Every day about this time, a red cardinal would fly into the yard and onto the birdfeeder/ Elaine hadn't seen the bird in a long, long time.

She continued to look out the window and daydream, when she heard the phone ring.

Walking into the kitchen to pick up the phone, "Hello."

"Is Elaine there?"

"This is she, who is this?" She asked, puzzled.

"Your mother," she answered

"How are you doing?"

"I should be asking you that, sweetheart," her mother replied.

"I'm taking one step at a time, trying not to think about him so much."

"You're gonna make it through this, I'll always do what I can. You're my child, I love you," she said.

"I love you too."

"Where's David?"

"He's at school," Elaine answered.

"So have you heard from Rudy's parents?"

"Yes, as a matter of fact. This morning on the way to take David to school," She answered.

"And?"

"They were acting real nice, as if they were up to no good as usual," she replied.

"Do you think they're up to something?"

"I wanna give them the benefit of the doubt, but something's telling me to stay on my guard."

"Just hold on to that instinct, nine times out of ten, you're right," her mother said.

"We'll see."

The two of them talked for hours about everything. This was always a wonderful thing no matter what either one was going through. Her mother had a way of getting her to smile in any situation. Like Elaine and her son, this was a bond no turmoil or person could break.

DAVID'S SCHOOL bus stopped in front of the house and let him off the bus. At the same time, Elaine opened up the door to greet him. This was a ritual she always did with her late husband. Simple, loving things like this, had become a major blow to her heart when she wasn't able to do them anymore with her husband.

She hugged David and gave him a kiss on the cheek. He gave her one back on the cheek. The two of them hugged each other tight. She took off his book bag and always checked to see if he ate his apple. As usual, he took one bite and put the rest back.

"Mommy, guess what I did today," he shouted.

"What, baby?"

Pulling the picture out of this book bag, "This is a picture of me, you, and Daddy."

With tears rolling down her face, "This is so beautiful, baby."

"Mommy, why are you crying?" He asked, touching her face.

"Mommy's just proud of her little prince."

"You'll be ok, Mommy, I'll take care of you," he said, hugging her.

"Now go and wash your hands for dinner," she said, giving him a pat on the butt.

The two of them were eating dinner, and usually his favorite.

She pointed over at the broccoli, trying to get him to eat it. She knew the only way he would eat it is with cheese. This was their little battle a couple of nights a week with vegetables. He usually won, or so he would think.

"You're the best mommy ever," he said.

"Thank you, but you still have to eat your vegetables"

"Oh, Mommy," he said, pouting.

He ate half of the vegetables and she was pleased. Tonight she won this battle and tomorrow night, it will start all over again. She glanced over at the empty chair where Rudy would always sit. She was remembering how he would always eat food out of her plate when her head was turned. David would always laugh when he did.

The phone was ringing and Elaine got up from the table to answer it.

"Hello?"

"You and your son need to leave town before the two of you get hurt," the voice said on the other end.

"Who the hell is this, how did you get my number?" she asked in a mild tone.

"What's wrong, Mommy?"

"Nothing, sweetheart," she replied, and hung up the phone.

The two of them finished up their meal and went to take their baths and go to bed. She put David to bed and made sure all the doors and windows were locked. Panic was starting to set in, but she had to stay strong for her son.

She went into her room and looked out the window at the moon in all its beauty. This was a tradition Rudy did. It meant more now that Rudy was gone, and it became her line of peace.

CHAPTER
FOUR

ELAINE GOT UP EARLY and went into David's room and he was gone. She started calling for him, but he didn't respond. Immediately she thought about the call she received the night before. She frantically ran into the living room, hoping he would be there. He'd get up early sometimes to watch cartoons, but the room was empty.

"David, David," She called out in despair, but still received no answer.

She ran outside to the backyard to see if he was in the sandbox, be he wasn't. There was a secret hiding place she knew he would go but she couldn't remember. On her way back to his room she was starting to remember. There was a door in his room that she had overlooked. This door led to the attic where he would play a lot.

Elaine quickly opened the door and ran upstairs. She got halfway up the stairs and heard his little voice. Tears poured from her eyes at the sight of him.

"David, baby, you scared Mommy," she said in relief, hugging him.

"Mommy, you can't interrupt the court case," he said with his little robe on,

"Mommy thought something happened to her little judge," she said, wiping her tears.

"I'm fine, Mommy."

"Okay, baby."

"We'll take a five minute break so I can talk to my mommy," he said, looking over at his toy robots.

"Mommy came to wake you up. but you weren't there, sweetheart."

"I always wake up early and play court because I wanna be a judge, Mommy, when I grow up."

"Mommy will love you and be proud of you no matter what you become," she said.

"I don't want you to be scared anymore, Mommy. I'll tell you when I play from now on," he said, giving her a big hug.

"Okay, baby."

She watched and smiled at him playing court with his toys. Of course he was always the judge in court. Elaine believed Rudy had first started the game with him. It was one of the many games the two would play.

The two of them went down to his room and watched some cartoons. David's stomach was starting to mumble and she knew it was time for breakfast. She looked over at him and smiled, glad to see his appetite didn't change.

"I'm going downstairs to fix you some breakfast, okay?"

"Some pancakes and sausages!" he shouted.

"Yes, David," she replied.

On her way down she heard a noise coming from the back door. She went back into David's room and grabbed one of his baseball bats. David looked over at her taking the bat, but didn't pay too much attention. She creeped down the stairs.

Her heart started racing as she slowly came down the stairs into the kitchen. The noises got closer as she moved more into the kitchen. She saw a tall man, broad shoulders with a black jacket, that looked familiar. He turned around. It was her brother. He'd always come in the kitchen back door and grab something to eat.

"Victor, what the hell are you doing?" She said, putting down the bat.

"I always come in through the back," he answered.

"This bat almost went upside down."

"Come on now, you wouldn't hit me," he said with a banana in his mouth.

"Intentionally, no, but I thought you were someone breaking in."

"Did someone try to break in?" He asked.

"No, but I did receive a crazy phone call last night."

"Who was it? What did they want?" He asked, looking back on the counter.

"Who they were, I don't know, but they wanted me to leave her with David," she replied.

"You think it has anything to do with Rudy's death?"

"Maybe, there have been a lot of strange things happening," she replied, leaning the bat against the wall.

Elaine went to the refrigerator, getting what she needed for David's breakfast. She looked over at Victor eating his banana, like he and David did a lot.

"Are you staying for breakfast?" She asked.

"No, I've got things to do today."

"Okay, I guess I'll see you later," she said.

Elaine closed the door behind him as he left. She and Victor were the closest of all the siblings. She always knew she could depend on him for anything. Along with her parents, he was her rock.

Later on she called for David to come down and eat his breakfast. He always came down with his judge robe on. Sometimes he would trip, but he never allowed anyone to help him up.

"Mommy, why did you take the bar downstairs?"

Hesitantly, "Mommy thought she heard something in the kitchen."

"Heard what?" He asked, eating his pancakes.

"It was nothing, eat your food, baby."

IT WAS three o'clock in the afternoon and there was a knock on the door. Elaine looked out the front door window to see who it was. It was her mother with packages and some food. She knew the meals weren't as nig when Rudy was alive and thought they needed it.

"It's me, your mother."

Opening the door and smiling, "It's you, I thought it was somebody else, Elaine replied.

"Who did you think it was?"

"It's nothing really," she answered.

"Dont' lie to me , I'm your mother," She said with her signature look.

"Why do you always say that?" Elaine asked, smiling.

"Because it always works, now tell me."

"Some things have been happening around here and it's starting to bother me," she said, closing the door behind her mother.

"Did someone try to break in?"

"I'll tell you when we get in the kitchen," she replied.

Elaine didn't want to discuss the conversation anywhere she thought David might hear it. He had a way of knowing things most kids would never pick up on.

"Let me take this and put it on the table," Elaine said, putting the food and package her mother brought on the table.

"So what happened?"

"Well the first thing is the car that was parked in front of the house with two strange men inside, the second is the phone call I received telling me that David and I need to leave here," she explained.

"Oh my god, did you call the police, baby?" Her mother asked.

"No."

"Are you crazy or something, why the hell not?"

"It was probably some prank call," she replied.

"Prank call or not, you need to call the police."

"They probably won't call again anyway," she replied.

"Promise you'll be careful and watch yourself and David, sweetheart," she replied.

"I will, I promise, are you staying for dinner?"

"Not tonight, baby, you know it's all about your brother on the weekend," she said.

"What do you mean?" Elaine asked.

"You know, the sports; football, basketball, and even golf."

"Really?"

"Yes really, let me get back before he realizes he ran out of chips," she said smiling, grabbing her purse.

"Tell him I said hello and I love him."

"You need to come over more. and bring David too."

"I will," she said, giving her mother a kiss and a hug.

"Give him a kiss for me, okay?"

"You know I will," she said, opening the door for her mother.

She watched her mother get safely into her car, waving good-bye. Her mother paused and looked at her two babies, worried someone was out there trying to hurt them. Although Elaine sometimes said it was crazy how her mother worried about her, she was glad her mother cared. The two didn't always get along when she was young. As Elaine got older her mother understood her a lot better.

When she first Married Rudy, her whole family was a little hesitant. Shortly after the marriage, they opened up more. Normally this wouldn't have been a problem, but the families weren't ready for someone in their camp to be in love with someone from another race. Especially if the two of them were of opposite races.

It took her father a little bit longer to love and respect him, but it eventually came. Her mother has always told her and Rudy, he reminded her of a charming and handsome Bill Clinton, but without all the scandal attached.

She remembered the first dinner he was invited over to her parents house. Rudy was so nervous he kept playing with his fork. He ended up dropping it on the floor, and coming up from the floor, bumping his head on the table. Victor looked over and grinned at her father. He waited to see what her father would do, or worse, say.

Being the motherly woman Tempie was, she tried assisting him to see if he was alright. Elaine saw the reaction on her father's face and knew it couldn't be good.

The rest of the dinner went well and there was even a mild conversation between her father and Rudy. Victor felt a little left out, but got a couple of words in. He didn't particularly care for Rudy. or the marriage to his sister. Elaine always tried to get the two of them to talk.

Later on, Rudy and Victor got closer and learned to respect each other, if not love each other. Elaine found this to be pleasing even if it wouldn't last long. the two of them would routinely have mild conversations here and there before Rudy died.

Having stopped reminiscing, Elaine went back into the living room to check on David. He was lying on the bed laughing at the television with his beautiful smile. Sometimes he would change the channel to see what else was on.

The dishes in the sink were piling up, so Elaine went into the kitchen and started to clean up. This was an area where Rudy and David spent all of their time. After cleaning up the kitchen she made herself a cup of coffee.

She took the coffee into the living room and walked over to the wall where the pictures were. Elaine took her hands and ever so gently rubbed the picture of Rudy holding David when he was a baby.

Suddenly there was a knock at the door, "Elaine, are you there?"

It was her neighbor, Alexis, from next door. She didn't too much care for her, but tolerated her. The woman was always coming over, even in the rain. Alexis was old and none of her children ever bothered coming over. Rudy always told Elaine the three of them had become her children.

Elaine went to open the door, "Hello baby, how's everything?" Alexis asked.

"I'm doing fine, how are you, sweetie?"

Elaine knew this usually led to thousands of questions. She'd always bring food over saying it was nothing to prepare. The dishes were always elaborate and didn't taste too bad. Alexis was always dressed to kill when she did come over.

"So what do you have there?"

"Oh this was nothing, just something I whipped up right quick."

As always, Elaine was on cue, "Let me take that from you, come in and have a seat."

"I love what you've done with the place," she said looking around as if it was her home.

"Mommy, is that food on the table?" David asked.

"Yes, sweetie."

"Who made it, Mommy?" He asked.

"Ms. Johnson from next door, do you want a taste?"

Shaking his head, "No way, Mommy."

Elaine quickly rushed David out of the kitchen and gave him

a smirk. It wasn't necessarily condoning his behavior, but it was funny. Alexis got offended and felt a little small.

"I'm sorry about David, he is a young child learning about life," Elaine explained.

"That's okay honey, my nieces and nephews weren't exactly angels all the time."

"So how's everything at the company these days?" Elaine asked.

"Well after my husband died I'd rarely get time to myself."

"What about your kids, don't they help?"

"Yes, but only in the office. I've never had that at home, they're all too busy for me," She said with tears rolling down her face.

Holding her hand, "I'm sorry to hear that," Elaine said sincerely.

"Well let me go back over, I hope you enjoy the dish."

"Thank you."

"You're welcome."

Elaine decided to try this red, spaghetti-like dish. She took a bite and actually swallowed, and gave it a good nod. It turned out to be a good dish. Elaine had a plate of what looked like tuna casserole. The trick was to get David to eat, but she wasn't holding her breath.

CHAPTER
SIX

LATER ON THAT MORNING, Elaine was going through some papers in her bedroom. She saw an old envelope that she didn't recognize and wondered what was in it. She pulled a document out of the envelope that looked like a financial statement. THere were other documents as well as a disc labeled "Family Pictures' '.

Elaine decided she would look at them later. The phone rang suddenly, making her jump. The items were put back in the envelope and laid on the bed.

"Hello?"

"Is Mrs. Devant there?" The voice asked on the other end.

"Yes, who is this?"

"I knew your husband ma'am." the voice replied.

"A lot of people did, what's your name?" She asked.

"I can't talk to you like this, they may be listening in."

"Who the hell is this and who are they?" She asked angrily.

"I'll be in touch," the voice replied, hanging up the phone.

Elaine slammed the phone down, running to the window. Looking desperately out the window, hoping to catch whoever it was outside. She was going out of her mind wondering why now all of this was starting to happen. David was oblivious to it all, or so she'd hope.

That afternoon, the two of them left the house and went to the park. This was a regular thing with the three of them every Saturday. Now that the two of them only went, it was different. The three of them had a special place in the park near the weeping willow tree near the pond.

"David, Mommy's gonna get some ice cream, what kind do you want?"

"I want chocolate and strawberry, Mommy," he replied, throwing rocks into the pond.

"Two scoops, David?"

"Yep, I'm a big boy, Mommy," he answered.

"You stay right there, Mommy's gonna go get it."

"Ok, Mommy."

A few feet behind her was an ice cream vendor, surrounded by other parents. They were all frantically trying to buy the popsicles, ice cream sandwiches, and ice cream cones. Elaine looked over her shoulder and saw David move over towards the big rocks.

A stranger came towards David, holding a piece of paper in his hand. He was about six foot one, a hundred eighty-five pounds, brown eyes, and was casually dressed.

"Hey little man, is your name David?" The stranger asked, slowly walking closer to him.

Turning around and looking at the stranger, "Yep, how did you know my name?"

"I knew your daddy, would you do me a favor little man?" The stranger asked.

"I'm not supposed to talk or take stuff from strangers," he said, moving back.

"But I want–"

"Mommy, Mommy!" He screamed, running away.

Elaine heard the shouting and quickly looked over to see David running towards her. She saw the stranger and quickly ran towards David. The stranger made eye contact with her and quickly took off running.

"David, are you alright?"She said, holding him tight.

"I'm ok, Mommy."

"What did he do to you?" She asked.

"Nothing, but he had this piece of paper in his hand."

"What kind of paper, honey?"

"I don't know. Mommy," he replied.

"Mommy's going to take you somewhere else to get ice cream, baby."

"Okay."

Elaine drove to the grocery store and picked up some ice cream and cookies and went home. The two of them got inside the house and saw the mail on the floor. She shut and locked the door, and kneeled down to pick up a letter, and saw a letter addressed to her husband. This was odd because her husband had stopped receiving mail about two months ago,

There was no return address on the envelope and it was black. This was disturbing and demanded her attention. She took the bags to the kitchen and put them down on the counter. Elaine ripped open the envelope. Rudy's initials were at the top of the paper. Her heart started racing as she started reading the letter.

The letter had been written in crayon, a deep, dark red color. She was almost afraid to read it, but did.

"You and your son need to leave before you get hurt. The things you have, you don't deserve and will be taken from you. This community would be better without you. If you and your son want to see his next birthday, I suggest you leave."

Elaine's heart started racing and she quickly went into the kitchen and threw the letter away. She closed all the curtains, locked the doors and took David upstairs to wash his hands for dinner.

The two of them were in the bathroom washing their hands, Elaine kept thinking about the letter, and who was trying to harm them. She'd thought about whether or not the man in the park was responsible. The thought of sending David away had crossed her mind, but decided not to.

"Mommy, what are we eating for dinner tonight?"

"Mommy's going to order a pizza and you can have anything on it," she answered, gently grabbing his nose.

"I want everything on mine, Mommy."

"Okay, baby."

CHAPTER
SEVEN

ELAINE WAS in the kitchen fixing David's breakfast before Church. Looking out the kitchen window, she saw her mother walking through the backyard. She always made sure David went, even if Rudy and Elaine didn't. ELaine smiled as she was coming through, thinking she was on time as usual.

"So where's my grandbaby, and why are you dressed like that, you're not coming are you?"

"Yes," Elaine said with a big smile.

"Is the world coming to an end or what?" Her mother shouted, smiling.

"No, not yet anyway," Elaine replied.

"Well, it's good to have some of the family going," her mother said, touching her face.

Elaine thought about the many times her mother would try so hard to get her to go. She once got them to go, but she had to plan it. Elaine was getting David ready as usual when she got a phone call. It was her mother and she told her there was an emergency at her home.

The three of them got there and it turns out that her mother said she sprained her ankle. Her mother insisted on going, being a devoted Sunday church-goer. Rudy helped her to the car, and drove to the church. Elaine wondered why her father wasn't there to help.

They all got out of the car and walked her mother towards the church. Just as they made it inside, it started raining like there was no tomorrow. Suddenly, Elaine noticed her mother was walking okay and her father was at the door smiling.

"I guess you'll have to stay for the service," her father replied with a devilish grin.

"Did the two of you plan this?"

"Everything but the rain, and you know who did that," her mother replied, sitting down on the pew with David, smirking.

Elaine finished up in the kitchen and the three walked out the door. She made sure she locked the door, hoping for no surprises later. They walked through the yard, heading to the car, when Elaine noticed she forgot her keys.

"I'll meet you at the car, I forgot my keys," she said, heading towards the house.

David looked out on the streets and saw the stranger he met in the park coming in the yard. He came closer to David and his grandmother.

"Remember me, David?" he said, looking around.

His grandmother quickly grabbed him, "Who are you?"

"My name is Cisco," he replied, looking around the yard.

"Does my daughter know who you are?"

"No, not yet, but it is important that I speak to her though," he replied.

"Look, if you're the one who's been harassing my daughter, I'm calling the police."

"Ma'am, Ma'am, I'm not here to hurt anyone, especially your daughter or her son."

"Let's say I believe you, why are you here?" She asked.

"To save her and her son from being killed."

"I think you'd better go, before I call the police," She said, moving her and David back.

"Okay, just give her this," he said, handing her a videotape and walking away.

The stranger walked away quickly, leaving the yard. Elaine came out the door and saw the man, now running across the street. She walked towards her mother wondering what was going on.

"My keyes were upstairs on my bed, what's going on?" she asked.

"Don't be scared, but that man running across the street was in the yard."

"Oh my God, are you and David alright?"

"We're fine, he said he was here to save you and David from being killed," her mother answered.

"What?"

"Mommy, it was the same man in the park, remember?" David shouted.

"He didn't do or say anything crazy, did he?"

"He wanted me to give you this tape," she replied, handing her the videotape.

"I hope to God, this hasn't anything to do with the phone calls I've been receiving."

Elaine put the videotape in her purse and the three headed to church. While the three of them were in church, Elaine noticed some of RUdy's family. Predominantly, the church was black and considering how they felt, this would have been the last place they'd be. Sunday service was almost over and not a moment too soon. Elaine was starting to doze off.

There was a tap on Elaine's shoulder, wanting her to wake. "Elaine, ELaine, wake up, the service is over."

"No, no, stay away from us," Elaine said, asleep in one of the pews.

Elaine woke up in panic, looking around for David. Rudy's parents looked on in shock.

"Elaine, relax. It's okay, honey. David's with me," her mother said.

"I had this terrible vision of someone coming into our home trying to kill us."

"My God, Elaine, are you and David gonna be alright?" Her mother asked.

"We'll be fine," she said, getting up from the pew.

Elaine looked and saw David's grandparents coming over. She hoped they weren't here to cause a scene, because she was clearly not in the mood. Her mother saw that look on her face and moved herself and David out of the way.

"Well, well, the good Lord must be running a two for one special into heaven," Elaine said, smirking.

"Elaine, we didn't deserve that," David's grandmother said.

"You deserve that and more, but we're in God's house."

"We didn't come to make a scene, we just wanted to see our grandson."

"Where was all this when me and your son offered to bring him over, but you were always too busy?" She asked, raising her voice.

"We've offered visitations to see David."

"Why, so you can put stuff in his head about what a terrible mother I am?" She replied, shouting even more.

"Look, Elaine, we tried to be civil with you about this, but we're done now," his grandfather replied.

Elaine rushed outside where her mother and David were. The rest of the congregation looked on, as Elaine walked briskly down the stairs, heading towards the car. David's grandfather ran after Elaine, into the street to her car.

"My lawyers will be sending you something in the mail," he shouted.

"Go to hell, you better hope it happens before the two of us die," she said, getting in the car.

"What?"

"Yes, someone's been threatening us all week, or didn't you know?" She replied, giving him a dirty look and driving off.

ELAINE LOOKED in on her mother and David in the sitting room. David and her always enjoyed spending time together. Her mother looked up at her, and saw the worry in her eyes. Elaine went to the kitchen, and started to make herself some tea.

Putting her hand on her daughter's shoulder, "It's going to be okay"

"Yeah. I wish I could agree."

"You've been through worse and you came out fine," her mother said.

"If you're talking about Rudy's death, that was different," she said.

"Nevertheless, you'll make it through this."

Her mother went back to where David was and played some more. Elaine went back to the kitchen and prepared an early meal for the three of them. She was curious as to what was on the videotape.

The garbage can was full and was starting to smell up the kitchen. Elaine took the garbage out, thinking about how her man did that every night. At the dumpster there was a stick she used to prop the top open.

She propped the lid open and started emptying the garbage. When she was done she bent down to pick up the can and saw a man kneeling on the side of the dumpster. The voice whispered, "Don't scream and run away. I need to talk to you."

Backing away from him, grabbing the stick, "Give me one good reason why I shouldn't gouge your eyes out with this stick," she asked.

"Because I'm about to become your guardian angel," he answered.

"Are you the man in the park from the other day?"

"Yes, my name is Cisco."

"How do I know you're not trying to harm me and my son?" She asked.

"If I wanted to, I've had more than enough chances to do so," he replied.

"I still don't believe you, but I have no reason not to either."

"Fair enough, at least I look at the video and my cellphone number is on the video."

"Ok, but this still doesn't mean anything," she said, briskly walking back to the house.

The stranger quickly ran down the alley. Elaine locked the door behind her, having a temporary sense of peace. She locked the house up and went upstairs to her bedroom to watch the tape. Her doubts lingered about what the stranger had said, but owed it to herself and David.

The video came on and the stranger's face was the first thing she saw. He was a tall, hispanic man, fairly handsome, with brown eyes and curly hair and wire glasses. She was tempted to turn the video off, but her gut told her to watch and listen.

"Hello, Mrs. Devant. I'm a friend of Rudy's. Rudy and I were working on a business venture together before he died."

Elaine thought this was a little odd, considering she knew a lot about his business partners.

"The project was two high rise apartment buildings adjacent to each other. He had told me this was it for a while. That night he was at the site, making sure things were done right.

I know the evidence and autopsy said he died accidentally falling off one of the beams, but he didn't. He was pushed.

I know this because he called me to let me know he was there. I know you're saying how did I get on the site? Well, Rudy was the only one with the key.

He gave me a call and asked to come by to go over some things. I said sure, grabbed my flashlight, and headed there.

I arrived at the construction site's front gate and the gate was open. When I got to the trailer office, the door was open but he wasn't inside.

So I walked to the actual site and heard someone shouting. I went further in and I could make out Rudy's voice, but not the other two.

The shouting got louder and suddenly I heard something fall in the shadows. I went over and pointed the flashlight in that area, and it was your husband.

I stayed with him until the ambulance came. I tried pointing my flashlight to see who the other two were, but they were gone.

I would've come forward earlier, but I'm not exactly clean cut in the construction business. But Rudy was willing to give me a chance. Besides, in this town, the police aren't exactly my friends."

The video went off and Elaine leaned back on the bed in shock and fear. She wondered if the two men he heard were the same ones in front of her house some nights ago. Once again, she checked the doors and invited her mother to stay the night, and she did.

CHAPTER NINE

A FEW DAYS PASSED. Elaine was grocery shopping, trying to not be gone too long and keeping her cellphone on. SHe was about to weigh some vegetables and felt a hand on her shoulder.

Scared to death, Elaine quickly turned around and swung the vegetables at whoever it was. It was the stranger on the video. His glasses came off and flew on the lettuce, where the guy working produce was.

Looking amazed, thinking the two of them were having a domestic situation, "Hey mister, here go your glasses," he replied.

"Damn, you might not need my help after that," he said, putting back on his glasses.

"What the hell are you following me for?"

"I take it you didn't see the video?"

Looking him straight in his face, "Yes, doesn't mean I believe a damn thing you said," she replied.

"Please, I'm telling you the truth. I feel like I should've done more to try and save his life."

"It's too late for that, but for arguments sake, let's say I believe you. Why did someone wanna kill my husband?"

"I have no idea, but whatever it was, it was huge," he said, looking around suspiciously.

"I hope it wasn't something illegal and people were hurt, because that may have been his punishment," she said, wiping her tears.

"I didn't know him long, but that was never the impression I got, he was good people."

"Maybe you're not out to kill me," she said, composing herself.

Coming closer to her, "So are we in this together?" He asked.

"Yes, it's not like I have a lot of options, but I still don't trust you.

CHAPTER
TEN

ELAINE PARKED the car on the side of the road and got out and started walking down the path. This was something she did at least once a week. While on the path, she always thought about the good times with Rudy. The path led to the top of the hill where Rudy's grave was in the cemetery.

She came to the grave and kneeled down and placed the rose gently on his grave. Her hands glided over his name and she closed her eyes, reminiscing about Rudy. A sudden breeze passed over her whole body, it was as if Rudy was saying hello.

She felt a hand on her shoulder and slowly opened her eyes and looked up. It was David, smiling over his mommy's shoulder.

"What are you doing here?" She asked.

Before David could answer, her mother replied "I brought him here. The teacher said she tried calling you to let you know they had received a call that his grandparents were picking him up."

"His grandparents!?" She shouted, rising from the ground.

"You know we only pick him up on Fridays and if there's an emergency," her mother replied.

"David, you know that thing Mommy asked you to do when grown-ups are talking, can you do it for Mommy?"

"Okay, Mommy"

David covered his ears and moved away and turned around. He would pretend he couldn't hear what was being said.

"David's grandparents are up to something, I know it was them that called the school," Elaine replied.

"Well if it's Bonnie and Clyde," Elaine's mother replied, seeing Rudy's parents coming up the path.

Elaine moved David behind her and her mother stood firmly by her side. The two of them got closer and Elaine could see Michael, Rudy's grandfather, with an envelope in his hand.

"Can't I have some peace and quiet at my husband's grave?" She shouted.

"Lucile, would you take David for a walk while we discuss something with you daughter?"

She looked over at Elaine to get the go ahead, "Yeah, but not far."

"I wanted to do this in person and not have it done by someone else," he said, handing her the envelope.

Elaine had a gut feeling it concerned Rudy, but hoped it didn't. She opened it up and pulled out a petition for joint custody of David.

"What the hell is this!?" She screamed loudly.

Lucile and David looked over at the three when they heard the shouting.

"We told you we were going to do this, don't look so shocked," he replied.

"Your son hasn't even been dead a year and you're already pulling some bullshit like this?"

Her heart was racing and the fear of losing her son and the bond they shared was too much. Tears started rolling down her eyes.

"Look, Elaine, we believe you're a good mother, but we will prove otherwise where our grandson is concerned."

Suddenly, with all her strength, she slapped him in the face.

"You kiss my ass, you son of a bitch," she replied, ripping up the petition, causing his white face to turn red.

"I can't imagine why my son ever wanted to marry you," his wife said.

"I can give you two reasons. One, we were in love with each other and we wanted to spend the rest of our lives together. Two, he wanted to make sure he didn't end up marrying a no good bitch like you, at least that's what he always told me!"

Having seen what just happened, Lucile and David quickly walked back over to where the three of them were. She knew her daughter could handle herself in any situation, this was no different.

"Elaine, are you alright?" Her mother asked.

"Sure, we need to go before things get out of hand."

The three of them walked down the path, leaving Rudy's parents standing there, looking like fools. David innocently looked back at his grandparents.

The three of them arrived at the house, ready to relax after everything that happened. Elaine got out of the car and opened the trunk and started grabbing the groceries she bought earlier.

"David, sweetheart, come help Mommy with the groceries."

"Okay, Mommy."

"Elaine, are you sure you're alright baby?" Her mother asked.

"Yeah, I'm fine.'

"I'm just worried about the two of you going through all of this."

"If any harm comes to David, it's not us you'll have to worry about," she said.

"Come here, let me give you a hug, you look like you could use one," she said, embracing her tightly.

"David, come here and give granny a goodbye kiss," Elaine said.

"Okay," he said, giving her a big kiss.

"I'm gonna leave now, I love the two of you and be careful," her mother said.

"We will."

She started walking down the street and waved goodbye. Elaine and David waved back. Her parents only stayed two blocks down the street, but seemed a long way. David used to say they lived at the end of the world because the blocks were so long.

The two of them got inside and Elaine quickly locked the doors behind them. She decided to cook David's favorite because one, she was tired, and two, franks and beans were easy. It was one of the few nights David could eat a little junk food.

CHAPTER
ELEVEN

IT WAS two o'clock in the morning and Elaine heard a crash downstairs. She rushed down the hall to David's room, hoping he was alright. He was still sleeping when she busted the door open, fearing the worst. She quickly went to his bedside and gave him a kiss on his forehead.

She saw a flickering shadow on the wall of his room and saw that some shadow on the other side of the door. Walking towards the door, she smelled smoke and saw flames. Elaine went back in and frantically woke David up. The two of them rushed down the stairs, hoping to beat the fire.

The two of them made it downstairs into the kitchen, where she called for help.

"Community emergency, how may I help you?"

"My house is on fire!" Elaine answered Frantically.

"Calm down, ma'am, is there anybody else in the house with you?"

"Yes, my son."

"You and him leave the house immediately and an emergency vehicle will be there as soon as possible."

"Okay."

Elaine and David quickly ran out of the house with the

phone dangling. They ran out the back door, because the flames had pretty much taken over the front of the house. The two of them got to the front and saw all the surrounding houses with their lights on.

People were coming out of their homes in their bedclothes, staring at the burning house, as if it was a light show. The firetrucks and paramedic soon showed up, frantically rushing to the house.

Pulling on his mother's nightgown, "Mommy, why is our house on fire?"

"I don't know sweetie, but Mommy won't let anyone hurt you."

Driving up the street, Lucile saw Elaine and David standing in the street. She parked the car in the next door neighbor's driveway and got out.

Running over to Elaine and David, "Are the two of you alright?"

"Yes, we're fine," Elaine replied, tightly hugging her mother.

"What happened there?"

"I heard a crash and I jumped out of bed and ran to David's bedroom, then I saw a flickering light and smelled smoke soon after. I got David, we ran downstairs into the kitchen, and called for help and came in front," she explained.

"Ma'am, are you alright?" One of the paramedics asked.

"I'm a little startled and shocked."

"Sit down, ma'am," he said, helping her to the curb.

The fire chief was walking over to Elaine, hoping to console her. "Ma'am, is this your house?"

"Yes, it is," she said, looking up at him in desperation.

"Ma'am, do you have any idea what may have caused the fire?"

"No, sir," she replied.

"From what we can tell, it started in the front of the house downstairs."

with tears rolling down her eyes, "I know I didn't leave anything on."

"Well, as soon as the dog sniffing team gets here, we'll know for sure."

"Thank you for keeping us informed," Lucile replied.

"You're welcome."

"Elaine, Elaine," her next door neighbor yelled as she was walking across the lawn with a blanket.

This was the one time Elaine didn't mind seeing, not because she had a blanket, but because she may have seen something.

Wrapping the blanket around Elaine, "Are you and David alright, honey?"

"A little scared, but we're okay," she replied.

"Ms. Johnson, did you see anything peculiar going on?" Elaine asked.

Being careful to answer, "No, I actually saw nothing peculiar."

"Are you sure?"

"The only thing I saw was a stray dog taking a dump on Mr. Williams' lawn when I peeped out the window."

"Somebody must've seen something," Elaine replied.

"If they did, they're probably all too scared to say anything."

"Elaine, think about it. Rudy's family owns half the city of St. Louis, and if there's any idea they're involved, people are keeping shut," her mother explained.

"Speaking of the devil, look who's coming up the street."

It was David's grandparents coming out of their limo, looking shocked at half of the house almost being burnt down.

"What the hell happened, Elaine, and is David alright?" His grandfather asked.

Holding him close by her side, "Me and David are doing fine."

"What the hell happened?" He asked again.

"I heard a loud crash and I woke up and frantically ran down to David's room, turns out he's alright, but I saw shadows flickering off the wall and quickly realized the house was on fire, I grabbed David and we got out."

"As long as my precious grandson is okay, I'm okay," his grandmother replied.

Elaine couldn't believe her ears as to what she just heard.- Forget the fact that she too could've lost her life and two families would've lost their loved ones. This is typical of the two of them, she thought to herself, but this was the icing on the cake.

"David, cover your ears," she asked.

"Okay, Mommy."

"Do you motherfuckers ever stop? Do you ever stop with the insults, threats, and the unwanted visits, huh, do you?"

"Can't you see that you and your robot for a wife are upsetting my daughter?"

"Lucile, this is between your daughter and I, okay?" He said, pointing his finger at her.

"Don't point your finger at me, you son of a bitch. Our grandson, my daughter, has been through hell, she's lost her husband, his father, she's been getting threatening phone calls and now someone's trying to kill them. This is between all of us now," she shouted with her breathing increasing.

While this commotion was going on, Elaine managed to look over at the arson team pulling up with their dogs. There were three men barely out of their twenties, taking charge of three German Shepherds. Elaine would soon find out what caused the fire, if not who.

A couple of hours passed and the sun was now rising. Surprisingly, none of the neighbors went back inside their homes. To Elaine, this must have been a nightmare come true.

"Mrs. Devant," the fire chief said with a regal voice.

"Yes?"

"The dog sniffing team did a thorough job of the fire and found this," he said.

"Is that what I think it is?'

"If someone was trying to harm you, this definitely would've did it," he replied, showing her the molotov cocktail.

Elaine's fears came back when she looked at the half broken bottle. She knew whoever it was, they were determined, now more than ever, to get rid of her and David.

CHAPTER
TWELVE

A COUPLE of days passed and she was now living with her parents. Something her mother had insisted on, forcing her to reconnect with her father. She dreaded this happening, because he was always bringing up the past, and not in a good way.

Sitting in the den in his man's chair… or his throne as she and her brother called it, Elaine watched from the door.

Looking up at her from his newspaper, "Are you gonna come in?"

Smiling and being bashful like when she was a child, she walked in. It was like the first time she ever walked inside. He had books from every decade, except for ones that required him to have an open mind and be liberal.

"I'm glad you and David are alright," he said.

"I appreciate that."

"Did they say what caused the fire?"

"Someone threw a molotov cocktail in the front window," she said, sitting down on the couch.

"None of your neighbors saw who may have did it?" He asked.

"Apparently not."

"You and David are always welcome here, I hope you know that," he said , smiling at her.

"I know, but it's nice to hear you say it," she replied.

"I know I haven't been there for you, helping you deal with Rudy's death and I'm sorry for that."

Elaine was stunned and pleased at the same time to hear her father utter those words, and it was something of a miracle.

"Yes, even I know when I've been wrong and made mistakes," he said.

"How much time do we have left?" She said, walking towards her father.

"For what?"

"The world must be coming to an end," she replied, laughing.

"You get me, baby girl."

Elaine couldn't believe she and her father were laughing and bonding.

"I know me and Rudy started out bad, but we were getting closer before he died."

"Yeah, he told me now and then the two of you conversated about things," she said, smiling.

"So can we start over, and may I get a hug from my baby girl?" He said with tears rolling down his face.

"Always."

"I love you, Elaine."

"I love you too, Daddy."

The two of them held each other tight and cried. He had his little girl back, and she had her dad back in her life. Things were once again the way they used to be.

Coming into the room with David, "Well hallelujah," Lucile said with joy.

The two of them looked over at Lucile with tears still rolling down their eyes. He waved her and David over to get in on the hug.

"Grandad, doesn't Uncle Victor want a hug?" David asked.

"He probably would if he was here David," his grandfather replied.

This was too often the case no matter what was going on. Elaine and Victor often spoke on how their dad rarely showed affection to them. Maybe he figured if their dad didn't, why should he. This had always bothered Elaine, but she had her own issues with her relationship with their father.

CHAPTER
THIRTEEN

IT WAS one o'clock in the afternoon and Elaine was in her parent's kitchen when the phone rang.

"Hello?"

"May I speak to Elaine Devant?" The caller asked in a low voice.

"This is her, who is this and why are you talking so low?"

"It's me, Cisco, forgive me for sounding too mysterious, you never know who's listening."

"What's that noise in the background?" She asked.

"I'm in some restaurant downtown using the payphone."

"Sir, are you gonna order something?" The waitress asked.

"Excuse me."

"What are you gonna have to eat, drink , you know, stuff like that?" She asked, raising her eyebrow.

"What does it matter, I'm on the pay phone?" He replied nonchalantly.

"You're in a restaurant where waitresses, much like myself, are working our asses off to get a tip," she said, tapping her pen on the pad.

"I'll take a cup of coffee," he said quickly, hoping she would leave.

The waitress walked off and he'd hoped Elaine was still on

the phone. He realized she was in no mood, after having her house almost burnt down, to listen to someone she barely knew.

"I'm sorry about your home."

"Even you knew."

"How can I not know, you're the widow of a man who's one of the richest men in the state," he said.

"You've been doing your research I see."

"Not to mention you were the head nurse in the number one hospital in the state," he explained.

She was bothered by how much he knew of her. This wasn't something that brought him any closer to her or David. Knowing nothing about this man was one wall she was going to get over quickly.

When Rudy was alive he would always tell her they were fortunate to have the things they did, so enjoy them. She always helped others with gaining their fortune, now she needed to help herself, stay ahead of the game.

"So what did you call me about?"

"Do you know anything about your husband's family business?" He asked.

"Only that they own a lot of warehouses and different plants, why do you ask?"

"Can we meet somewhere?"

"Yeah, I guess, in a public place," she answered reluctantly.

"Okay, how about Union Station downtown?"

"That's fine, give me half an hour," she replied.

"Okay, I'll see you in thirty."

Elaine walked out knowing she had to make one stop and this may give her the leg up on Cisco. She wasn't one for all the deception, but there was a lot to lose.

She arrived at her destination, there was a lot of traffic inside. The place was full with ladies in their best and some in their worst. The men weren't any better, some were drunk as all get out.

Elaine saw her friend looking at one of the ladies. She could see the woman was trying to persuade him. Chase, of course, wasn't having it. Apparently he'd dealt with her before and knew what was up.

Walking closer to his desk, she was always impressed by her friend and how he always made it through. The two of them went to school with each other, and she was like his big sister, body guard, and of course, friend, all in one.

"Come on, Chase, give a working girl a break," the lady asked.

"Samantha, if I give you a break , all the girls will want one."

"Well whaddya know, a cop who's actually a good one."

Chase looked up and saw Elaine coming towards him, he had a big smile and his whole face lit up as if he was a kid on his birthday. Most of the time this only happened when Elaine was around.

Rising up out of the chair, "Long time, no see."

"Yes, it has been a while," Elaine replied.

"Sit down, Elaine, have a seat."

"I hope I'm not bothering you by coming here, but I need a favor.'

"Before we get to that, how are you holding up?"

"Rudy dying so suddenly and the way he did was a shock, but I'm making it," she replied.

"Good to hear/'

"I see these ladies are keeping you busy today."

"All the time, what can I do for you, Elaine?"

"You're a good friend and I've always respected you, but I can't tell you why I need your help, but I do."

Being a serious cop like he was, we weren't sure what to say or do after that.

"Come on, you just can't expect me to help you and not tell me what I'm getting into," he said with overwhelming curiosity.

"Chase, trust me, I know how this must look, but it's important. I wouldn't ask if it wasn't," she said, looking around in the squad room.

"Answer me one question and I'll help you."

"Okay."

"Does this have anything to do with your house almost burning down a week or so ago?" He whispered.

Elaine nodded and Chase gently grabbed her arm and walked her over to the coffee machine. "I'd be careful, Elaine, Rudy's father has been down here asking the chief if he can get some officers to tail you."

"For what?"

"Well, it's no secret you and that bastard don't get along."

"It's bad enough he tried to embarrass me at church, now this."

What's he after, Elaine?"

"My son and my sanity, if I'm not careful."

"What the hell are you talking about?"

"He's trying to take my child, by suing for joint custody."

"Why in the hell for? You're a good mother," he replied, sipping a very dark cup of coffee.

"Well at least I've got you in my corner, Chase."

"Always."

"Thank you."

The two of them walked back over to his desk and discussed why she was really there. The two of them grew up together and always talked about doing crazy and ambitious things. Being a cop was one he'd thought he might do, but didn't know if he had what it took.

Elaine always as a friend supported what Chase did, no matter what. Telling him she was marrying Rudy was hard for her, knowing how Chase felt. He took it well and remained her good friend throughout the marriage.

"I need to be somewhere, so I hate to rush you, but I need some information," she said.

"What kind of information are you looking for?"

"It's on a guy named Cisco."

"Let me guess, a Hispanic male, tall, brown eyes, and curly hair?" He replied.

"Yes," Elaine answered.

"His name is Cisco Velasquez and he's not exactly welcome in the construction business.

"Why?"

"Let's take this outside, away from wandering ears," Chase said, looking over at one of the new rookies.

"Your mystery guy was involved in one bad construction job and almost went to jail."

"Was he stealing?" She asked, hoping for a more detailed answer.

"No, he got in over his head on one particular job and cut some corners that lead to fraud, or so they say."

"He told me he wasn't exactly welcome in the city," she explained.

"The man was trying to establish himself in the construction business and was reputable until.."

"Until what?"

"Until , and a lot of people say things were being done on one job in particular behind his back."

"So someone was setting him up?" She asked.

"Yeah, pretty much he was securing a lot of contracts and he always was good to his men and even gave bonuses when work was done on schedule."

"Sounds like he was a good man and a good boss."

"He was. but here's the crazy part. One day he was visiting a supposedly finished job when the upper levels of the building collapsed," Chase explained.

"My God."

"THat's not all of it, some people saw guess-who's limo parked across the street."

"My father-in-laws."

"Yes."

"What interest would my father-in-law have had in it?"

"Well, Elaine, your father-in-law had a huge construction business and apparently didn't want any competition."

"Rudy never told me about that specific part of the business."

"Your father-in-law was into underhanded business practices."

"But how could he not know things were going on on that site, it was his job to know, he was the boss."

"The men believed in treating people who worked for him with respect, and he received the same respect. So there was no need to think wrong doing was going on…" he explained.

"That concept is definitely lost on my father-in-law."

Giving him a kiss and hug, "Thank you for all your help, Chase."

"You're welcome, here's my number if you need anything, and Elaine, be careful. Your father-in-law is a dangerous man."

"I'll keep that in mind," she said, walking to her car.

Elaine was glad to have found out the things she did to be better prepared. Although Chase basically said he's a good man, Elaine still wondered what was up.

One thing that was really bothering her about all of it was the fact Cisco waited so long to come to her with this information. She assumed his life may have been at risk, if someone saw him on the construction site that night.

Elaine arrived at the meeting place and waited at the top of the escalator for Cisco. She thought waiting for him at the top of the escalator, she could see if she was with anyone.

The two of them looked at each other and advanced towards each other. Elaine came from the escalator, focusing on his every move, and he hoped she would listen without hesitation.

"Any particular reason you wanted to meet me here? I would've thought you might've wanted to meet me somewhere quieter," she said.

Cisco knew at this moment she wasn't going to be manipulated easily, not that he would've, be he's met his share, "I just thought you might like this better," he replied.

"Me, I can be seen in public, you're the one on the run."

"You get right to it don't you?"

"Yeah, I do," she replied.

"Let's get some coffee," Cisco suggested, directing her to the stand behind them.

"How do you take it?"

"Cream and a little sugar."

The two of them sat down at the table and slowly started drinking their coffee. Elaine looked in his eyes as if she could really see what was going on inside. He was overwhelmed with her natural beauty and of course her directness. Rudy always told him she was outspoken, and ready for anything or anyone.

"Now what's this about my In-law's business?" She asked.

Looking around, being careful of suspicious strangers, "He had a lot of lucrative businesses besides the front business," he explained.

"You mean the construction business, I thought that was a legitimate business, and where all the money came from ," she said, looking confused.

"The man's not beyond venturing into other areas for money."

"I don't know why I'm so surprised, I once heard him tell Rudy once that if they didn't get enough money from a construction job, he knew how to pick up the slack," she explained.

"So what then?"

"Rudy looked confused and asked his father what that meant, his father then told him not to worry about it."

"Well if it's any consolation, Rudy has always been an honest guy as far as I knew," he said.

"I'll never believe my husband knew or was involved in illegal activities."

"Did your husband ever tell you about the Omega project?"

Just as Elaine was about to answer, she saw her father-in-law coming towards them, and with him, his two seven-foot bodyguards. She wasn't worried so much about herself, but for Cisco, if her father-in-law remembered him.

"Well, well, my whore for a daughter-in-law, oops, or used to be," he replied, blowing smoke in her face.

"Today must be Annual Asshole Day and you're leading the parade," Elaine replied.

"I can see why Rudy liked you, you're so feisty."

Elaine looked him over and wondered why a bastard like him would smoke a cigar, while wearing a five-thousand dollar suit. I guess it was nothing to him, after all, he was worth millions. He always told Rudy in the past 'If you can't show the millions, why have them?'

"Yeah, and for the life of me, I can't understand why you're still married," she said with a smirk.

"Your friend looks familiar, haven't I seen you around town?"

Standing up from the table, "No, that's impossible, I'm poor," Cisco replied, leaving the two of them to work it out.

Michael, her father-in-law, looked over her shoulder, eyeing Cisco as he went down the escalator. He knew he'd seen his face before and wasn't going to let it go. He never forgot a face, and in his position in society, he couldn't afford to.

"Who I keep company with is none of your damn business," she shouted in hearing range.

"That's where you're wrong, sweetheart, any strangers in my grandson's life is my business," he replied.

"Don't you have somebody's life you can go ruin?"

"No, not yet anyway, but I'm working on it," he replied, helping himself to the other chair that was left empty by Cisco, "I'll get serious with you, we're getting closer to having to go to court."

"Look, I'll tell you one more time, you're not taking him from me."

"Quit overreacting, we're not trying to take him from you,

we want joint custody," he replied again, blowing smoke in her face.

"I don't care how much money you have, or who the fuck you think you are, but I'll fight you all the way," she said, rising up off the chair, looking him in the eye.

"With what?" He asked.

"With every penny I've got."

Elaine walked off, now and then looking behind her, keeping him in her sight. She had an overwhelming need to get to David. Now more than ever, finding out what her new friend knew was deadly important. This only added to the money problems and it was going to get worse. There were one of those days she expected Rudy to say things would get better, but she knew she'd never hear it again.

CHAPTER
FOURTEEN

A WEEK HAD PASSED and Elaine hadn't heard from Cisco and wondered if he was still among the living. The thought of him risking his life to give her information to save hers didn't sit well with her. No thoughts of where he lived or anything came to her. She'd hoped Michael, her ex-father-in-law, hadn't remembered his face or where he saw him.

Coming down the stairs quietly, as not to disturb Elaine, "Look, Mommy, I dressed myself, look," David shouted at the end of the stairs.

Looking over at David from the living room couch, "Mommy's gonna show you the right way," she said with a big smile.

She walked over to David and saw he had his shoes on the wrong foot, pants and shirt inside out, and his belt was on backwards. He always said when he grew up to be a big boy he would dress himself. These were one of the moments she'd wish Rudy was here to see. The two of them always laughed at Davids little 'I'm a growing boy, no?'

The phone rang in the living room, causing Elaine to leave David to deal with his little clothing disaster.

"Hello?"

"Is this Elaine Devnant?" The voice asked on the other end.

"Yes, who is this?" She answered.

"It's me, Cisco, are you alone?"

"No, I haven't heard from you in a while, where have you been?"

"Do exactly what I say. Go up to the upstairs window and look down the street, and tell me what you see," he asked.

She quickly went upstairs, not to let on to her parents and David what was going on.

"Elaine, are you there?" Cisco asked frantically.

Slowly pulling back the curtain, "I'm here, I'm looking right now."

"What are you doing, Mommy?" David asked curiously.

"Hold on one second, my son's at the window," she said.

"Mommy, what are you looking at?" He asked again, waiting for an answer.

"Mommy's looking at some birds outside the window," she replied, hoping that would be enough to satisfy his curiosity.

"What kind of birds?"

"Peeping toms," she answered, still haven't actually seen anything herself.

"I've never seen those kinds before, can I see, Mommy?"

"No, I'll show them to you next time, but you can go and tell your granny I said give you some cookies," she said, giving him a kiss.

"Yay, cookies," he shouted, running to find his grandmother.

"Okay, he's gone, I see a red car and a black car with no plates," she said.

"The red car belongs to your parents' neighbor and it's empty, it's the black car with the two gentlemen in it is the problem," Cisco explained.

"I haven't noticed it before," Elaine replied.

"You should've, they've been there all week since you and David moved in with your parents."

"Oh my God, what if they try to hurt somebody in my family," she said hysterically.

"Calm down, Elaine, anything that they haven't done already they're not going to do, at least in broad daylight."

"Should I call the police?" She asked, still looking out the window.

"Yes and no."

"What?"

"You're going to call your friend Chase, the one who you were asking about me, to call the nearest officers around and give them the street address where the car is parked and tell them they're selling drugs out of the car," he explained in detail.

"That's never going to work, they'll know I made the call."

"Not if you call on your cell, if you have one?" Cisco said.

Elaine didn't know if this was an insult or a suggestion. In this day and age, who didn't have a cellphone or two?

"That doesn't happen in this neighborhood," she explained.

"You're a woman in her thirties and, I believe, well-educated, tell me you know better than that."

"Yeah, I guess you're right," she replied.

"You're also going to call the owner of the house –Mrs. Williams, I believe that's her name– where the car is parked in front of and make an excuse for her to come out at the same time," he explained.

"So you want it to look like she called?"

"See, you're beautiful and intelligent."

"Thank you, I think," she replied, hanging up with him and grabbing her cellphone.

Elaine followed Cisco's instruction to the detail, letting the police know exactly, details themselves and getting Mrs. Williams out of her rocking chair outside. She never thought she'd ever lie to the police or put an old woman in danger, but these were rough times. This wasn't the time to worry about it, and she didn't.

The police had gotten there in five minutes, yes five minutes, this was Brentwood. If they didn't get this quick, someone was going to hear about it. This neighborhood was one of the best on the outskirts of St. Louis. On the same token, they probably ignored a lot because it was Brentwood.

Elaine could see the police walking up to the car slowly and cautiously. Here came Mrs. Williams right on cue.

One of the officers stopped and turned and walked towards her, "Ma'am, were you the one that called about two men selling drugs out of their car?"

"Drugs? In front of my house? Oh good lord, I've never seen those men before," she replied, looking overwhelmed at all the commotion.

"Are those two men right there?" The officer asked politely.

"I didn't call the police, but maybe I did, I can't remember. I'm old, things aren't clicking the way they used to, officer," she answered, scratching her head.

The other officer was now looking at the driver from the side of the car with his right hand on his piece. His partner walked back to the car and took the passenger side. While this was happening, Elaine looked on, thinking how impressed she was with herself for pulling it off.

The officer on the driver side waved the driver out, as did the officer on the other side. The officer asked for I.D. and had the two gentlemen spread 'em. They were escorted to the sidewalk after being frisked. One of the officers was running a check on the I.D.s and found nothing.

Coming out of his squad car. "You guys are clean, lucky for you," the officer said.

"So we can go?"

"Not until you tell us why you're parked here," the officer said, looking down at him.

"We were lost and stopped to figure out where we were."

"Well how about we escort you to where you're going, you'll get there faster," he suggested.

"Sure," one of the gentlemen said. "That would be good."

The officers knew they were lying but couldn't hold them for anything illegal. The lack of plates, maybe, but it could be easily fought in court.

"Oh, and fellas, I suggest you not be in this neighborhood, or any neighborhood, without plates and directions," he replied, getting back in the squad car.

"We'll do it, sir, thanks for the escort."

"To protect and serve, fellas, to protect and serve," the officer replied, putting on his shades.

LATER THAT EVENING, Elaine and her family were getting ready to have dinner when the doorbell rang. She was hesitant to answer the door, especially after what happened earlier. Who or whatever was behind the door, she was determined to hold her head high.

Pulling back the curtain, she saw that it was Cisco, she quickly opened the door and gave him a smile, as if she had just seen an old friend. Cisco stood there, returning the smile, as if she were an old girlfriend who he still cared for.

"Come in, I don't wanna leave the door open for too long, give'em something easy to shoot."

"Elaine, who is that at the door?" Her mother shouted from the living room.

"A friend of mine," she replied.

Jumping out of his chair, "I'm going to see Mommy's friend," David said.

"David, come back here to this table," his grandmother shouted.

Elaine had her back turned. closing the door, when she heard David running. Turning around, she saw David give Cisco a really hard kick in his leg.

Cisco gave a look of sharp pain and wondered how a little

guy like that could kick so hard. He figured he must've scared the kid in the park and the kid remembered.

"David, what are you doing kicking him?" She said, grabbing his hand and gently pulling him away,

"That's the man stranger from the park, he came here to hurt us," he said standing in front of her, giving Cisco a mean look.

"I wouldn't hurt you or your mommy," Cisco said, kneeling down in front of David.

"What about my granny and grandaddy?"

"Them either."

Looking up at his mother, "Mommy, is he telling the truth?'

Elaine smiled down at her little man protecting her, "Yes he is, sweetheart."

"Okay, but I'll be watching you mister," he said, walking away, taking a look back.

Things like this had happened before with David after Rudy had died, but usually he defended her from the bag boys at the store who said she was pretty looking.

"Good kid, as long as he's around I gotta feeling you'll be alright," he said, smiling.

"Yeah, he's growing up fast and just like his father," she said.

"Is that a good thing?"

"Ninety percent of the time, the other ten percent he's a handful."

"Something smells good."

"We were just about to eat, would you like to join us?" She asked, looking down at his stomach after hearing it growl.

"I don't wanna impose."

"You may not, but your stomach does," she said again. This time, the both of them heard his stomach.

"Sure."

"Let's go eat," she said, taking him down the stairs to the sunken down dining room.

"Everybody, this is Cisco, an associate of mine."

Her parents looked at him, then at each other, both

wondering if he was an associate or the new boyfriend. True to his word, David kept an eye on mister Cisco, giving him one of his Daddy's you-better-not-do-anything-wrong looks.

"My daughter says you're an associate of hers, what type of an associate?" Her dad asked, leaning back in his chair at the table.

"Dad, he's–"

Interrupting her, "He can talk for himself, or are you his interpreter?" Her father asked sarcastically.

"We got together and discussed rebuilding the part of the house that burnt down," he replied.

"Are you a contractor or something?"

"Yes and no, " Cisco replied.

"What is it with you young people, you can't give a straight answer anymore," her father said, shaking his head.

"I used to have my own construction business before someone sabotaged it."

"Did they sabotage your business or were you just in over your head?"

"No Sir, it was definitely sabotage, and hopefully one day I'll be able to prove it," he answered, looking over at Elaine, hoping she would believe him.

"Honey, do you have any idea who may have done it?" Elaine's mother asked softly, wiping David's face.

"I believe it was Michael Devant, and–"

"David, cover your ears," Elaine said, looking down at him.

"Okay, Mommy," he replied with his mouth full of food.

"I'm not surprised, that son of a bitch is a manipulative, back-stabbing, underhanded, deceitful bastard who uses his money to destroy lives," her father said, breathing heavily.

"Brian, calm down, your blood pressure will rise, honey," his wife said, gently grabbing hold of his arm.

"Daddy, calm down, as low down as he is, that's David's grandfather and he doesn't need to hear that," Elaine replied.

"I'm sorry if I've caused any problems with your family Elaine."

"Sweetheart, this whole family knows who causes the problems, and it's not you," Lucile replied.

"You were saying something about Michael Devant."

"Yes Sir, as I was saying, there was talk that Michael Devant was involved," Cisco replied.

"Elaine, come and help me bring the dessert to the table," her mother asked, giving a suspicious look.

Grabbing David's tiny hands, "You can stop covering your ears now, me and your granny are getting dessert. You be good."

"Okay, Mommy."

Elaine and her mother grabbed their dishes and headed down the hall to the kitchen. Memories of when she was little, going down this hall, going to the kitchen, getting some cookies, quickly came back to her. Although this time none of that was about to happen, and she already knew what it was really about. Dessert wasn't the only thing that was going to be served.

"Sweetheart, shut the door behind you and put the dishes in the sink. Oh, and what the hell is going on?" Her mother said, looking at her with a pie in one hand and the other waving about.

"It's not what you think and it's definitely not what Daddy and David think," she replied.

"Well, tell me something because I know you're lonely, but we've never even met him before this."

"Momma, we're not running off and getting married."

"Well if you do, can we at least buy you a wedding gift?" Lucile replied sarcastically, cutting the pie.

"He's helping with something important and it's long overdue."

Her mother looked at her, shocked at what she said, "I thought you said–"

"No, not that, Momma," Elaine said smiling.

"Well, whatever you're doing, if Michael Devant is involved, you've got to be careful," her mother said gently, rubbing her face.

"We'd better get in there before David starts an assault on the kitchen."

"David can wait, did you hear what I said, Elaine?"

"Yes, Momma, I will be careful."

The two of them walked beside each other with the slices of pie and coffee. The last time they did this together, Rudy was still alive, and they were bringing cake out for David's birthday.

"How's everybody doing in here?" Lucile asked.

"The three of us are doing fine and will be doing better soon as we get some of that pie," Brian answered.

"Let us get to the table first, Dad."

"Mommy, can I have two pieces?" David asked, swinging his legs under the table.

"No, and stop swinging your legs before they come off," Elaine said.

"Mr. Cisco, is that true?" David asked with his mouth full of apple pie.

"Looking at Elaine before answering, "Yep, because your mommy used to be little," Cisco recipe.

"Did your legs almost come off, Mommy?"

"Almost, but your granny told me to stop swinging and they didn't come off."

David wasn't quite sure if they were telling a story or the truth. It didn't matter, he was so into the pie he thought about nothing else.

Cisco was shocked to see the kid was talking to him and not giving him the I'm-watching-you look. He figured he scored a couple of points with Elaine when he answered the kid the way he did. This didn't mean 'welcome to the family', but it did mean the two of them were making progress towards trusting each other.

Brian was looking at the two of them staring at each other,

"Well if you need work or something, let me know, I'll get you in touch with Victor, my son."

"Elaine never told me she had a brother," Cisco replied.

"He's the oldest," her father replied.

"Does he not come to the family dinners?"

"Yeah, when you can catch up with him, if he's not busy with one of his women," Lucile said.

"You know men need their time to relax and plant roots."

"Ooohh, Grandaddy, you in trouble now," David said, grinning.

"Excuse me?" Both of the women replied simultaneously.

"I mean, he needs time to just kick back and get quiet time."

Brian knew this was a good save, or maybe because Cisco was company tonight. Lucile shook her head and gave him one of her okay-mister looks.

Elaine daydreamed for a minute about many interesting nights like this at her and Rudy's dinner table at home.

"Thank you all for the dinner and dessert, but I have to be going."

"Well, it's nice meeting you, young man, and good luck to you," her father said, giving him a firm handshake.

"Would you like something to take home? I could have a plate made for you," her mother said something.

"No, that's okay, I really have to get going, but thank you," Cisco replied.

Elaine walked him to the door, wondering if she'd ever see him after tonight.

"Take care of yourself, Elaine, I'll call tomorrow, and keep this door locked."

"I will, I was thinking about going back to the house and staying there now that they're almost done fixing everything," Elaine said.

"That's not a good idea, especially with someone still trying to kill you out there."

"Yeah, there is that," Elaine replied.

Giving her a wink, "Have a good night."

"You too, and be safe," she replied as he was leaving.

Elaine shut the door, looking out the window as Cisco left. She watched him walking towards a black sedan, looking behind his shoulder every few steps. A part of her wished she could've walked him to the car, but knew it wouldn't be wise. He got in safely and drove off down the long road.

IT WAS the morning of the joint custody hearing, Elaine and David were eating breakfast. She looked over across the table at David and wondered why someone would want to hurt him. Thoughts of her father-in-law did cross her mind, but dismissed the idea. After all, David was a part of his son whom he lost and loved a little.

David was making egg mountains with his food at the same time his mouth was stuffed. This was another dumb routine he and his father did.

"What are you thinking about, Mommy?" He said with a face covered in syrup.

"Nothing for you to worry about, sweetheart," she replied, gently wiping the syrup off his face.

"Are you ready , Elaine?" Her father asked, coming into the kitchen with his best suit and newest tie.

"As ready as I'll ever be I guess," she replied, giving her father a doubtful look.

"I want you to know whatever happens, your mother and I will be here for you and David."

"Hey, Granny," David shouted.

Lucile walked into the kitchen wearing a long black skirt with a split and a silk top. Her parents were the epitome of being young at heart. Some people even thought Lucile was Elaine's big sister when the two of them had girls night out. Her father stayed in the gym regularly, he even went with Rudy a few times.

"I appreciate you guys coming with me, I need all the support I can get."

"You're our daughter, we love you. If we didn't come we'd be no better than David's grandfather," her mother replied, giving her a kiss on the forehead.

"What judge in his right mind would give them joint custody of David, unless they were paid off or something," Elaine replied.

"Let's hope the good Lord has taken care of that if that is the case," Lucile replied.

"It will be fine, Elaine, you're a wonderful mother and everybody that knows you know it," her father replied, pouring himself a cup of coffee.

"If something ever happens, I know."

"Don't even say it, because you're going to be fine and so is David, now eat, sweetheart, you'll need it," Lucile replied.

"What would I do without the two of you?"

"You'll be just fine, we know that for sure," her father answered.

The four of them sat at the table enjoying the calm before the storm that would follow at the hearing. Breakfast was done, the four of them were heading out the front door when Elaine heard the phone.

"Dad, would you start the car while I get the phone?" She asked, standing in the doorway.

"Alright, let's go everybody."

Elaine went into the living room, trying to hurry and catch the phone before it stopped. Brian and Lucile were heading towards the car and David hopped in the back, thinking it was another ride. Brian looked into the rearview mirror and saw David without his tie on.

"David, I thought you had your tie tied?" Brian asked.

"Mommy said she was going to do it, but she forgot," he replied, shrugging his shoulders.

"Hello?" Elaine answered.

"Elaine, it's me, Cisco. Listen, it's important," he replied with an urgent tone.

"I'm on my way with my parents and David to the hearing, how did you get this number?"

"It wasn't easy," he replied.

"Brian, can't you tie his tie, because my arthritis is bad?" Lucile asked.

Looking down to find his seatbelt, "I can barely tie my own with my hands."

"David, be a good boy and go back in and tell your mommy to tie your tie," Lucile asked.

"Granny, I have to use it," he said, crossing his legs.

She looked back at him shaking her head, "Okay, let's go, David."

The two of them got out of the car and headed towards the front door. David was walking faster than normal for obvious reasons, Lucile could hardly keep up.

"Elaine, did you notice anything unusual last night?" Cisco asked.

"No, why, what's wrong?"

"I watched the house the other night, just to be safe and–"

Cutting him off, "I appreciate it, but you're only one man , you've got to look out for yourself," she said sincerely.

"I'll keep that in mind, but listen, those same two guys who were watching your house earlier were around last night."

"So you think they–"

Suddenly she heard a big boom out front. it was so powerful the window blew in the living room. She quickly hit the floor, dropping the phone. Fear came over her as to what would happen next. Quickly rising off the floor, she headed to the door,

"Oh my God, David!" She screamed out the door, observing the explosion.

"David, David!" She screamed out with fear.

The smoke cleared, she saw something closely resembling a body on the lawn. Fire along with smoke was coming out of the car like a coal furnace. She quickly ran to the lawn, hoping her fears were just that. It was David and her mother, face down with Lucile's arm over David.

Frantically she shook the both of them, hoping, "David, Momma, wake up!"

"Mommy, Mommy," David said, slowly coming out of his stunned state.

"Oh my God, Mommy's here, baby, Mommy's here," she replied, kneeling and grabbing David.

"Elaine," Lucile sighed, barely moving towards Elaine.

"Momma, thank God you and–"

Suddenly she realized her father wasn't with the two of them.

"Momma, Momma, where's Daddy?" She asked.

With her head now resting on Elaine's leg, "He's in the car, He's in the car!" She screamed.

She tried getting up and crawling on her knees to the car, hoping for a miracle. Elaine pulled her back in fear of something happening to her mother and hugged her tightly.

"No, no, he's Dead!," Her mother screamed.

Elaine held on tight to David and her mother, terrified at what just happened. Thought of her father immediately rushed through her head and the special day they had reconnecting that bond. Thoughts of her father-in-law's face also came rushing through her head but for a whole different reason.

The smoke was dark and hot and caused all the neighbors to come out and stare. They were already nosey, but this was the biggest thing since the Wilsons down the street bought their new mercedes.

"Someone call the police!" Elaine shouted, barely holding up David and her Mother.

She took the two of them inside the house, all three still in shock and were coughing furiously. The three of them walked in the den and sat on the floor. Elaine made a desperate call to Chase, her long time friend at the police station.

The station was busy with loud voices coming from everyone shouting and screaming. Most of it was coming from the suspects, hookers, and yes, some of the officers who had to be heard all the time.

Having just had an uncomfortable meeting with his Lieutenant, Chase heard his phone ringing on his desk, "Hello?"

Breathing heavily, "Chase, oh my God!"

"Elaine, what's wrong, what's wrong?" He repeatedly asked.

"The car, the car!" She shouted.

"Calm down, Elaine, what about the car?"

"There was an explosion at the house, the car blew up with my father in it," she answered, gasping for air.

"My God, Elaine, I'm so sorry, I'm on my way."

Chase left the precinct, gathering up as many of his colleagues as possible, at least the ones he could trust, on the way to Elaines.

Elaine locked all the doors in the house, attempting to prevent anyone else from getting hurt. Visions of the explosion were racing through her head like a bad nightmare. Had this been a nightmare the pain would be over by now. Regrettably, she was awake and it was all too real.

Ten minutes had passed since she called Chase, but it felt like a week in her state of mind. He banged on the front door hoping that the worst hadn't happened, death. "Elaine, It's me, Chase, open the door," he said, panicking that there would never be a response.

The curtain near the front door moved slightly, revealing Elaine's fragile hands. The door opened up and she embraced Chase, holding on tight. "The car blew up and my dad was inside, David and my mother barely survived," she replied with tears running down her face.

"Where's David and your mother?"

"In the living room, scared to death."

The two of them walked towards the living room, hoping together they could calm the two of them down. The room was massive and full of modern and old furniture.

"I thought you said they were in the living room," he asked, looking around, puzzled.

Elaine walked over to the south end of the room and put her hand behind a lamp shaped like a dragon and the wall had opened. Chase walked behind the wall and saw Lucile with tearful eyes, gripping David tightly.

"Lucile, we'll find who did this and bring them down," he said, gently placing his hand on the two of them.

"You won't have to look far, it's that bastard of a grandfather of David's," she said with deep hatred.

"Momma, stop, David doesn't need to hear that," Elaine said.

"Elaine, my husband just got blown up in a car, possibly by your father-in-law and almost killed me and David. David's going to hear a whole lot of shit today," her mother replied, wiping her tears away.

"Everybody calm down, we'll get this figured out. Elaine, let me see you in the other room," Chase said, hoping to talk privately about what just happened.

The two of them walked through the living room to the door, all the while keeping an eye on the secret room, "Is your mother right? Could he have done it?" He asked.

"I seriously doubt it."

"Why?"

"That bastard hates me but, I never thought I would say this, he loves David and would never want to see him hurt or dead."

"Then who else could have done it?" He asked.

Running her hands through her hair, she came up with one name, one she didn't want to mention. She knew if she said it out loud, it could ruin her chances of finding her husband's killer.

"Tell me it's not your friend Cisco?" He said, gently grabbing her arm.

"No, of course not, everything that's been going on, I'm just trying to think clearly," she replied, turning her head.

Elaine knew he wouldn't do this under any circumstances, she wasn't sure about a lot of things, but this was one of them.

"Are you telling me the truth?"

"Of course I am, I've never lied to you before, have I?"

"No," he said, giving her a hug.

"Thank you for coming, I know I'm getting you deeper and deeper in all of this."

"It's been kind of slow downtown anyway," he said, smiling.

She looked up at him and always liked the fact that even in situations like this, he managed to crack a joke and a good one at that.

"I'll leave some men here to watch over you and the two of them."

"Yes, that would be good, especially while my mother is here."

The two of them started to walk towards the door when they heard footsteps behind them, "Bye, mister Chase."

Bending down, "Hey little man, how are you doing?"

"I'm doing good, I'm gonna protect Mommy and Grandma," David said, looking up at Elaine, smiling.

"I know you will, little man," Chase replied.

"Let me walk you out. David, you go back to the room with Grandma," Elaine said.

"Okay, Mommy."

"Elaine, You're gonna need to get a few more locks on these doors."

"I'll have it done tomorrow," she said, reassuring him.

He walked out the front door and waved his men to come closer and get a briefing. He made sure he moved to the sidewalk so Elaine couldn't hear. "Listen up, no one is to go in and out but Elaine, her mother, and David, is that clear?"

"Boss, you want one of us to stay with the family?" One of the officers said, extending his broad shoulders.

"One, no that won't be enough, we'll need at least four of you. Two in the house and two outside.

Chase looked around at the people gathering and looking at the explosion and wondered who, out of all of them, either knew something or planted the explosion. He had his officers question the crowd, but each one of them were signaling to him with a head nod that no one was telling anything.

The crowd started to whisper while a limousine pulled up to the house. Elaine saw this through the window and was not shocked who came out of the limo. It was her mother-in-law, dressed to the nines, as if anyone cared.

Elaine went back into the living room, shutting the door behind her, and went into the secret room. "Momma, keep David in here and don't let him out no matter what."

"What's wrong?"

"The in-laws have shown up, or at least Rudy's mother," she replied, walking out the room, closing the entrance.

There was a knock on the door and Elaine was not looking forward to who was on the other side.

"What the hell are you doing here?"

"I'm here to see if my grandson is alright," she said with one foot already inside.

Elaine gave her the benefit of the doubt, she did after all, come by herself. This was really unusual for her mother-in-law since she never did anything without her husband's approval. The woman had lost her son after all, maybe she was coming to realize what was really at stake and putting her pride aside.

CHAPTER
SEVENTEEN

WALKING ONTO THE CONSTRUCTION SITE, he was heading towards Rudy's trailer when he noticed the lock on the door had broken. Hesitantly he approached the trailer, gently kicking the door open, being careful not to leave any fingerprints.

The Place had been ransacked; papers everywhere, chairs on the floor, and spilled coffee. The answering machine was blinking, indicating there were messages. He thought to himself, whoever was in here didn't think to delete the messages; mistake one. The second one, ransacking the place, more than likely overlooking what they possibly came for. The third and classic mistake, getting caught.

A car pulled up, it was unmarked, the men that came out weren't cops and he'd seen his share. He quietly slipped out the back of the trailer and ran into the ghostly, unfinished building.

Having made sure he was out of sight, he looked back and saw one of the men go back to the trunk and get a can of gasoline. The two men pulled their guns and entered the trailer. A few minutes later the men ran out, jumped in the car, and drove away. The trailer exploded.

This was the middle of the day, whoever did this had guts

and must've been paid a lot. He wondered if this was some of Rudy's old competitors or something more personal.

THE FIREMEN HAD FINALLY PUT the fire out and the bomb squad started to look for the cause. Chae couldn't understand why all this was happening to a good woman like Elaine.

"Hey, Lieutenant!" The Captain of the bomb squad yelled.

Chase walked over to the Captain with smoke still coming out of the car behind him. "What's up, did you guys find something?"

"We're not out here for nothing."

"Since when?" Chase replied.

The two of them gave each other a familiar grin and continued the conversation. "Here's your problem, this plastic charge was connected to the ignition," the Captain said.

Looking down at the few pieces of wire and plastic left, Chase was shocked. "Who would go through all this to kill Elaine and her family?"

"How about her father-in-law?" The Captain replied.

"Considering their history, he may be the prime suspect, or maybe that's too easy," Chase said.

"Hey, is she looking for a new husband, because I'm single and–"

Interrupting the captain, "Look, would you just stick to the job," Chase replied, looking at him, giving him the once over.

"Elaine, may I have a seat?" Her mother-in-law asked.

The two of them walked towards the den and went in. Her mother-in-law noticed two policemen outside the window. One of the men rushed inside the house and into the den with his gun drawn.

"Freeze!" He shouted with his gun pointed at Elaine's mother-in-law.

"Stop, put the gun down, put it down, she's okay!" Elaine shouted.

"Oh my God!" Her mother-in-law shouted, putting her hand on her chest, gasping for air.

Elaine got on the side of the officer, reassuring both him and her mother-in-law that everything was okay, "She's my mother-in-law, she came over to see if my son was ok."

The officer slowly put his weapon back in its holster and took a deep breath. It was his first day on this assignment and he thought it might be his last. He was the youngest one and probably the one who would be getting all the shit, especially after this.

There were sounds of footsteps coming from the rear of the house and Victor walked in. Elaine was shocked to see him of all people.

"What the hell is going on?" Victor replied.

"This officer was just doing his job and scared the shit out of our relative." Elaine said with a smirk.

Her mother-in-law looked over at her, trying to cover up the grin on her face. She was not pleased with Elaine, not that this time was any different.

"Victor, where have you been?" His mother asked, coming into the room with David.

"Hey, Uncle Victor," David said, smiling, seeming unaffected by everything that's happened.

"Hey, little man, what's up?"

"Mommy and Granny are sad, cause Grandad went away."

"As soon as Uncle Victor heard, he came over," he said, kneeling on the floor, talking to David.

Elaine looked over at Victor, wondering where he'd been and why he would show up, always, at the right time.

Victor walked over to Elaine with no expression, with his arms open for a hug. "We've got to stay strong," he said.

"I'm glad you're here, Momma is a wreck and rightfully so, she's ready to put a bullet in my father-in-law.

"So where is she?"

"In the living room."

Victor never knew about the secret room and neither did her father. For some reason she never thought to tell him. She was pretty sure Lucile was out of the room by now. "I'm sorry for the trouble, Mrs. Devant," The officer said softly.

"It's okay, we're fine, you can leave. I'll be fine," Elaine replied.

"I'll let the two of you talk while I go check on Lucile."

"Mommy, can I go with Uncle Victor?"

"No baby, Mommy needs you here with me," she said, gently taking his arm.

"Like I was about to say before I had a pistol in my face, I wanted to tell you that I've had no part in it."

"After everything that you and your husband have put me through, you must be smoking something."

"Just cigarettes," she said, pulling one out of her clutch purse. There's something going on in the company that I found out."

Amazed that the woman had a mind of her own, Elaine couldn't resist. "You're not going to get in trouble with your husband, are you?"

"I see even in tragedy like this, you have a sense of humor," her mother-in-law said, lighting the cigarette.

"We don't smoke in this house."

"Always the perfect angels, aren't you, Elaine?"

"No, but my chances of going to hell are slim, unlike your-self, now what do you want?"

Suddenly there was a knock on the door. It was Chase. "Elaine, we found some explosives in the car," he said, holding an electrical charge in his hand.

"I've got to go, hopefully I can tell you later," she replied, leaving the room and slipping out the back door.

"Should I be asking?"

"I'd like to tell you, but she didn't say much," Elaine replied.

"The explosives we found were plastic and it was of a high grade."

"So what, that means whoever planted it had enough money to buy the best."

"It's a funny thing, the charge that we found to ignite it looks familiar."

"Familiar? What do you mean?" She asked, taking a closer look.

"Before I became a cop I did construction, we would help the demo guys set things up and it looks like the ones they used."

The major construction company in this state and the midwest was her father-in-law's, so it was no shocker she could be involved. Maybe the information from his wife would've made things clearer, but her and Elaine weren't exactly best buddies, so she couldn't find out.

CHAPTER
NINETEEN

THE FUNERAL HAD COME days later and it was a nice Saturday afternoon. A sound could hardly be heard, all thoughts were on this last day to say goodbye. Brian wasn't that old, but death doesn't discriminate. Elaine was wondering how she was gonna hold it all together for the family with everything going on.

Elaine walked out the kitchen dressed in all black with only her ring glowing of gold. There was a sound of little footsteps coming from the top of the stairs.

"Mommy, I got a suit on," David said, finding his little tie.

Elaine showed a lighthearted grin, shaking her head, observing his appearance and the fact he had his shoes untied, different color socks on, and different shoes, "David, you can't go out like that."

"I'm a big boy, I dressed myself today," he replied, pulling up his pants.

"Why didn't Grandma help you get dressed?"

Suddenly his face went into a sad expression, "Because she was crying in the burnt room."

He was referring to the room that the fire almost got before the firemen came. Elaine walked up the stairs and picked up David and went to find Lucile.

The silhouette of her mother sitting at the mirror could be seen through the crack of the door. She was also dressed but had a string of pearls on Brian gave her on their tenth anniversary. She sighed when she looked down at the pearls and started crying.

Elaine and David rushed in to comfort her, "I'm here, Momma."

"Me too, Gramma, I'll watch over you and Mommy," David said with his shoes still untied, trying not to fall.

Lucile looked down, smiled, and cried at the same time, "You've always been Grandma's big boy, haven't you?"

"Yep."

Elaine and Lucile looked at each other and smiled at their little man. Lucile could see so much of Rudy and Elaine in him.

"We'd better get ready," Lucile said, wiping her tears.

The back door downstairs had opened up and a tall figure of a man had come into the house. He creeped through the kitchen and into the hallway under the stairs leading to the front door. Slowly, he walked up the stairs and down the hall and saw David.

"Hey, I know you, you're the stranger from the park," David said.

Lucile walked out one of the rooms and saw Cisco in the hallway, "Who the hell are you?"

"I'm not here to hurt anyone, I just needed to speak to Elaine," he said softly, trying to reassure Lucile.

"Elaine, get here now," she hollered, grabbing David.

Panic came over Elaine, running out of the powder room, thinking God only knows what, "What's wrong , Momma?"

"Elaine, I need to talk to you," Cisco replied.

"This is not the right time to do this, we're on our way to my father's funeral.'

"Please, this will only take a minute of your time."

Grabbing Elaine's arm, "What the hell is going on?"

"I wish I could tell you but it's best that I don't."

Lucile was livid and couldn't understand why Elaine would be allowing this to be going on of all days. The last time she saw Cisco was at her house at dinner and was suspicious of him then too. She knew in her heart she raised a child who could take care of herself.

"Watch yourself, me and David will be in the room with the door open," she said, giving Cisco the if-you-hurt-my-daughter-I'll-kill-you look.

Cisco and Elaine walked a few feet away from the door, "I went back to the construction site last night," he said.

"That site hasn't been open since that night Rudy died."

"There are ways to get in," he said.

"I see your talents are endless, so what did you find out?"

Suddenly the doorbell rang and Lucile shouted from the room, "I'll get it."

After hearing that, Elaine knew she couldn't let her mother answer the door. Opening up a door in this house could lead to unwanted guests–to someone getting killed.

"I'm sorry, but we'll have to do this some other time."

"Okay, but we need to do this as soon as possible."

"I'm sure you know your way out," she said.

"Yeah, I think I can figure it out," he said with a smirk on his face.

CHAPTER
TWENTY

THE FOUR OF them were on their way to the funeral thinking of only getting past this horrible day. Victor had come and picked the three of them up for the funeral. His mother was shocked he even had a pair of dress shoes, not to mention a suit.

Elaine could see that Lucile was looking at him in disgust. She'd hoped that her mother and brother would get into it, but no such luck.

"Hey Victor, would you mind if I ask you a question?"

"No, go ahead."

Looking at him straight in his eyes, "Why is it that you can dress well for this, but can't manage to show up for a family dinner?"

"Why are you doing this now? Dad is dead," he said, changing tones.

"Because I wouldn't have to if you would've done it sometimes, and can you please slow down before we all go together?"

"You know what, Momma, you can drive the damn car, okay? Because I don't need all this shit."

"What you need is to be cut out the will and not be left a red cent."

"Momma, he didn't deserve that and you know it," Elaine said, moving to the front of the vehicle.

Victor looked at his mother in disgust and rolled his eyes. He knew his mother had issues with him but not like this. If he was looking for a good reason to hate her, this was it.

"Why is everybody fighting, Mommy?" David said, tugging on his mother's dress.

"The two of you need to stop, you're upsetting David."

"If our mother showed me a little extra love now and then, this wouldn't be happening," Victor said, looking out the window.

"Our father, your husband and David's grandfather, is dead, you should've got this resolved when he was alive," Elaine said.

"You're right, Dad wouldn't want this going on," Victor replied.

The arguing had stopped for now and they all continued to make their way to the church. The car pulled up and Lucile saw a stretch limousine pulling up inside the lot. There was no mistake as to who it was and what bullshit they were about to cause.

The four of them were getting out their tinted window black suburban when Michael approached. This little confrontation was needed like a bad case of chickenpox.

Again with the blowing cigar smoke, "I would've thought you would've showed up in a limousine," Michael said.

"We don't need to show the city of St. Louis and the world we have money by showing up in a limousine, we show it by building free clinics and homes for people," Lucille shouted.

"I always did like a woman with spunk."

"So I can end up like a fucking robot and hate seeing the sight of your face every morning?" She said, looking at his wife.

"Michael Devant, one day all of your shit will catch up with you, one day," a voice shouted coming from behind.

"Maybe so, but not today, and who the hell are you?" He said, turning around, blowing cigar smoke.

"I'm that beautiful woman's brother," he replied.

Lucile lifted her veil to see if it really was him. "My God, Omad, you're a sight for sore eyes."

"I'm here for you, sis."

"I remember you now, vaguely, at my son's wedding and funeral," Michael said again, blowing his nasty cigar smoke.

"Your son's only been dead a year. I would think you wouldn't want to be at another funeral, especially not of a family you so despise."

"I'm here to show support, besides, we Devants aren't like everybody else, we're strong," he said, blinking an eye.

"Me and David don't need– David, cover your ears– shit from you, but to stay out of our lives," Elaine said, holding on to David.

The family members and friends were walking in the church, getting settled and looking at who showed up and who didn't. Everybody was stunned to see Michael Devant and his wife take a seat in the back.

While this was going on, Elaine and her family were in a waiting room waiting to start the funeral. The room was hot, maybe that was on purpose, so you couldn't get too comfortable.

"Let's all try to get through this and have no arguing, please," Elaine said.

David walked over to the door and peeked out to see all the people getting settled and whispering. He saw every body in black and probably wondered why. Poking his head out the door, he saw his grandfather all the way in the back.

Poking his head back in, he shut the door and ran over to Elaine, "Mommy, guess who I saw?"

"Who, baby?" She said, fixing his tie.

"Grandad."

Elaine's first thought was that David was thinking about his grandad and maybe pretending he was here. She had always been told sometimes kids see things that adults can't because of their innocence, until he kept going.

"Grandad is gone to heaven, David"

"No, the other one, Mommy."

Lucile looked over, hoping she hadn't heard it backwards, "Elaine, what's going on?"

"Momma, don't panic, just stay calm."

"Elaine, what is it?"

"Michael's here," she said, holding her mother's hand.

"Why is he trying to destroy this family after all these years," Lucile said, clenching her necklace.

"I think it's just me, Momma."

"There's more to it than that, but today's not the day to tell you about it," she said, gently caressing Elaine's face with her hand.

Elaine continued to stare into her mother's eyes and wonder what she meant. She had never seen her mother get so calm throughout this whole ordeal.

"Is everybody ready to go in?" The pastor said as he gently knocked on the door and walked in.

The tone of his words made it seem almost okay that a loved one was leaving us. This, after all, was his job and he had to make a good impression. Brian wasn't one for going to church unless he was persuaded by guilt. How ironic this will be his last time going.

Everyone started to rise out of their seats when the deceased's family started to come out. At first glance it was just bodies in black, no clear description of who was there.

Lucile looked around and saw Michael at the back of the church, showing the lack of respect for her husband by staying seated. She knew the man was an evil bastard, but this was the icing on the cake. Even in a time like this, there was no rest for evil.

IT HAD BEEN a week since her father died and Elaine's house was remodeled and has a new house guest. Her mother had moved in for a while while the house remained lifeless without anyone walking its halls. This short lived peace of mind was something of a dream compared to the last couple of weeks.

Elaine felt a warm comforting hug from behind her, it was her mother, "So how did you sleep last night?"

"Not good, I tossed and turned all night, not having Brian in the bed with me," her mother answered.

"Can you go for some coffee?"

"Yes, Baby, that would be great and make—"

"I know, Momma, a whole lot of cream," Elaine smiled looking back at her mother, walking towards the kitchen.

Elaine was preparing to get the morning brew going when she heard a knock on the kitchen door. Immediately she grabbed a butcher knife out of the rack, pumped with adrenaline. She didn't want to alarm her mother and son, but didn't want to lose control either.

She went close to the door and grabbed the pull string on the door blinds and from the side of the door she took a peek. It was Cisco with a gentle smirk on his face, waiting to be let in.

Looking relieved and still holding the knife in her hand, she opened the door, "Talk about your surprise guest."

"I would've called but the phone might've been bugged," he said, walking in with a bag with a familiar smell.

"What's in the bag?"

"I thought you might like some of these croissants."

Suddenly she started crying and smiling at the same time. Rudy would always get them every morning from one of the bakeries downtown. Cisco looked up to see her crying and looking worried. He knew they were good, but were they so good she cried over them, or was it something else?

"That's nice of you, Rudy used to go out and buy them every morning for the two of us."

"I'm sorry I've upset you, I just thought you might like them, they're the best in town, everybody buys them. I'll throw them away if you want," he replied.

"Doing something like that wouldn't be good for your health in this home," she said, wiping her tears.

Cisco looked over at the counter where the coffee was and saw a little face looking out from the side. It was David with his zebra print pajamas and puppy faced slippers.

"Mommy, isn't that the stranger in the park?" He said standing behind Elaine.

"Yes, it's the stranger from the park, his name is Cisco," she replied -splashing his hair.

"You're not here to hurt us, are you?"

"No, little man, I'm here to help you and your mommy, I promise," he said smiling.

"Okay, but I'll be watching you, Cis– Cis– I can't say your name but I'll be watching you."

Elaine had finished making the coffee when Lucile walked into the kitchen, noticing the tall stranger she had only met once gave her a little startle.

"Hello, good morning, ma'am, I'm sorry if I startled you," Cisco said smiling.

David's mouth was filled with croissants, looking at his grandmother, waiting to see what she was going to say about the stranger in their kitchen.

Responding to what he said, Lucille looked him straight in his eyes, "You seem to do that a lot."

"I'm just here to make sure Elaine finds out the truth about everything that's been going on, including Rudy's death."

"So what do you know about it?"

"Well, me and Elaine were–"

Suddenly Elaine handed Cisco a cup of coffee, "Here you go, nice and hot!"

"Why didn't you let the man finish?" Lucile asked.

"We're handling things and the less you know the less I'll have to worry," Elaine replied, giving her mother a hug and a kiss.

"I'll leave it alone for now."

LATER THAT DAY, Elaine was going to pick up David from school when she saw her mother-in-law in the school parking lot. She was alone without Michael by her side, nervously lighting up a smoke. Her body movements were like that of a crack addict, nervously moving, paranoid about her surroundings.

"This is the second time I've seen you without your husband, did hell freeze over or what?" Elaine said, coming out of the vehicle.

"I see though all of this you haven't lost your sense of humor."

"With in-laws like you I had to," she said, raising her brow.

This wasn't a confrontation Elaine was in the mood to have, but was always ready for. Somehow Elaine got the sense that something else was going on. This was a look of a woman who had something to tell.

"Elaine, I've had time to think about things," her mother-in-law said softly.

"You can actually do that without your husband?"

Elaine took comfort in knowing as rich and powerful as this woman was, her sense of power had somehow eluded her when talking to her 'tramp for a daughter-in-law' as she often put it.

"I'm not here to cause problems, I'm here to make mensa before someone else gets hurt."

"You said you were here to help, let's hear it," Elaine said firmly.

"We need to go somewhere less conspicuous."

"There's a big playhouse on the side of the building, we can go in there," Elaine said, extending her hand for her mother-in-law to go first.

There was a knock on the door and Lucile had just finished making herself a cup of coffee when she heard the knocking. It was too early for Elaine to be bringing David home, she thought to herself.

———

She arrived at the door, peeking out the side window. It was a young, handsome, bright skinned gentleman in a nice suit and tie with a briefcase. She was puzzled about who he was and why he was there.

"May I help you?"

"I'm Gabriel Carrillo with social services, is this Elaine Devant's residence?"

"I need to see a badge or some kind of identification."

He reached inside his suit jacket and pulled it out slowly, being careful not to startle this woman who obviously was cautious about who came to her door.

"Can you come back later?"

"Ma'am, I have to speak to her about David and the custody case, coming back later would only delay the new assessment of the young David's living situation," he said politely.

Still unsure of his real occupation and his motives, she decided to check him out by calling an old friend. "Sure, you can speak to her when she comes, but you'll have to wait on the sidewalk," she said.

"You're kidding, right?" He replied.

"Does it look like I'm kidding?" She replied, looking him in his eyes.

He walked away from the doors, heading towards the sidewalk, shaking his head in bewilderment over what he was asked, This had never happened to him before with his other investigations. but this wasn't your average family, not by economic standards anyway.

Lucile picked up the phone and called a friend of hers downtown. She was looking for answers and hopefully would find them.

"Hello?" The soft voice answered on the phone.

"Racquel, this is Lucile, I need a favor."

Racquel Hamilton was one of the few females who had worked her way up in the city government without succumbing to the pressures of her male counterparts, not to mention having lost parents at the age of ten to a man on heroin in a car accident.

"I'm sorry to hear Brian died so terribly," she said sincerely.

"Thank you, I still can't believe he's gone from my life and this house."

"You're a strong woman, you always have been. Remember the time you chased down Robert Cassidy for running off with our homework in junior high?" Racquel said smiling, hoping she had made her friend smile.

"I see you haven't changed, you always did know how to make me smile."

"You're a friend in need, I'm here for you, girl. Now tell me what you need," Racquel replied.

"I got an unexpected visit from Gabriel Carrillo, he says he's from social services and came to the house to do an assessment. I need to know if he's on the level."

"Give me a minute to find out, hold on," she replied, calling a friend of hers who was the head of the department.

While she was waiting on the phone to hear from her friend, Lucile kept a watchful eye on her unexpected visitor. looking out the window, she could see he was determined to see Elaine and David, he'd decided to take a seat on the sidewalk.

———

She was face to face with her mother-in-law, a woman who never had a good word to say about her. Elaine decided to give her the benefit of the doubt.

"You've got five minutes, let's hear it," Elaine said assertively.

"I wanted to ask you a question first of all if I could."

Elaine couldn't imagine ever talking to her, not to mention answering her mother-in-laws questions, "What is it?"

"Do you believe people can change, I mean really change?" Her mother-in-law said, looking up at her with tears rolling down her eyes.

Suddenly the bell rang and immediately Elaine pictured David looking for her. As much as she wanted to hear this, and she did, David was the priority, "I've got to get David, we can finish this later."

"Ok, let's not wait too long," her mother-in-law said, giving her a smile.

The two of them walked out of the playhouse , pausing a moment to look at each other. Kindness wasn't something associated with her in-laws, but maybe, just maybe, this woman was turning human.

David came running out of the front doors with his Mickey Mouse book bag, "Mommy, guess what I did today?"

"What, baby?"

"I made this picture to send to Daddy in heaven," he proudly answered.

She wished he was older and could understand things better, but she didn't have the heart to break his heart. "It's beautiful, honey."

"How long will it take to get there, Mommy?" He asked, looking at her with those big green eyes.

"I'm not sure, baby, I'll let you know when it gets there."

"Okay Mommy"

She wished it were that simple, but knew it couldn't be. There were many days she wished she could talk to Rudy and ask what to do.

The two of them were going home when she stopped at the light and saw a tall figure of a man coming up the side of the car. She immediately locked the car doors only to find out it was her new found friend.

"I thought something had happened to you."

"No, not yet anyway," Cisco replied, smiling while looking around cautiously.

Shaking her head, "You do get around, don't you?"

"Can I get in?"

"Yeah, I'm sorry, just being aware of my surroundings."

"I see I'm rubbing off on you," he said, reclining his seat all the way in the down position.

"Just enough."

Cisco looked up and saw two big green eyes above him looking down at him. "Hey, little man, how are you?"

"Mommy?"

"It's okay David."

"I'm doing fine, how are you, stranger?"

"I'm okay, you can call me Cisco."

"Okay stranger Cisco, you want some bubblegum?" He asked, shewing his favorite grape gum.

"No, but thank you."

"David, don't eat anymore, you'll spoil your dinner," Elaine said , turning the corner.

"You do a great job raising him, Elaine."

"It's hard but he's my life, and I'll do whatever it takes," she said, looking in the rearview mirror at her wonder.

The car pulled up to her mother's house and Lucile came

running out the side entrance to the vehicle. She was surprised to see Cisco in the passenger seat. Normally she would've commented, but the present situation dictated she didn't/

"Elaine, there's some man from social services here to see you and David."

"What?"

"You didn't know?" Lucile replied.

The social worker walked over to the car as Elaine and her passengers were getting out.

"Ma'am, are you Elaine Devant?" He asked, reluctantly moving towards her.

"Who wants to know?"

"I'm Gabriel Carillo with the Department of Social Services."

"I wasn't told about a visit from your office."

"We don't always call, but I tried calling to make sure someone was home," he said with a firm tone.

"How do I know you're on the level with all this?" Elaine said, grabbing hold of David.

The phone started ringing from inside the house and Lucile moved quickly back inside to catch it before it stopped. It was her friend with the information she wanted or didn't want.

Lucile walked outside, not ready to tell Elaine the informant's news, "Elaine, he's on the level, a friend of mine confirmed it downtown."

"I assure you there's no child abuse or neglect when it's concerning my child."

"I don't mean to disrespect you, but I have to make the assessment for the court, ma'am."

CHAPTER
TWENTY-THREE

THERE WAS lots of hustle and bustle as usual in the precinct, but today Chase would be given the gift of opportunity to help his friend. He was wondering how Elaine and her family were doing and wondered how he could help. There was a package in the wastebasket, a red, small box.

He didn't remember receiving or buying anything and definitely wouldn't have thrown it away without looking. His instincts told him it was suspicious and shouldn't touch it, but then maybe it was something of a bread crumb.

Calling the bomb squad was his first thought, but would attract much attention. He had to do something, people would start wondering why he was acting strange. He grabbed the package out of the waste basket and discreetly walked into the stairwell.

Chase wasn't that religious, but did believe in a higher power, and hoped he'd been all prayed up and was on good terms with this power. He started unwrapping the package, still thinking it could kill him. Suddenly he got a feeling of calmness and fear left his body.

Lifting the cover of the box, he heard the door to the stairwell open, "Sorry to bother you, Lieu, but the Captain wants to see you."

"I'll be a minute."

"Is that a gift from your girlfriend, Lieu?"

"Mind your business, rookie," Chase replied.

"Sorry, Lieu."

The rookie walked back in with his head down in embarrassment.

Chase watched the door, making sure it closed and quickly opened the box and saw a key and note with handwriting he didn't recognize. He did understand the location where whoever wrote him this note wanted him to go and how to use the key.

He'd hope whoever sent him was helping to save his friend Elaine from being killed and killing everybody else around her. This was a man who all his career as a cop went on gut instinct, but this time he was driven by his heart, hopefully it wouldn't kill him.

"Lieutenant," the Captain hollered.

Chase quickly put the note away in his shirt pocket and rushed back inside. He picked up his stride heading towards the Captain's office, "Right here, boss, I had to step out and take care of something."

"Look, I don't care about your presents from your girlfriend or your mommy," he shouted, wolfing down a huge breakfast burrito.

Chase looked surprised at the comment the Captain made and knew the rookie was running off at the mouth. "Nothing like that, just something I had to take care of."

"Well guess we need to talk, close the door."

Chase knew the Captain never asked you to close the door behind you unless he was gonna tear you a new asshole. It was almost like an initiation thing that every officer in the precinct knew.

Chomping down on his burrito, he went to turn the television on–the only one in the whole precinct. He waved Chase over to the television. "I'm going to tell you something and if you're smart you'll only need to hear it once."

"What's that, Captain?"

The Captain pointed at the television, still wolfing down the burrito. His stomach was like a huge luggage but with no bottom. He was a bald man, beady eyes, and the most disgusting breath and teeth you'd ever want to see.

"I know your friend's husband, Rudy Devant was his name, he was a good man, not like his asshole of a father," he said, still chomping on the burrito.

"I take it there's some bad blood between you and him?"

The Captain gave him a stern look. "He's the worst thing walking on two feet, the man has ruined lives way before your friend's woes."

"I didn't know you felt that way about the man."

"Let's put it this way, If the good Lord were looking for someone to vouch for him, the fucker would go straight to hell."

Chase couldn't help but to laugh, he'd never heard anybody say anything remotely close to what he heard from the Captain. He looked over at Chase and gave him a smirk, but quickly went to his straight no-nonsense brick face.

"Do you get my drift, or do I have to spell it out for you?" He asked.

Chase nodded his head looking straight at the Captain's mouthing moving about a hundred miles an hour.

Turning the volume up, the Captain started talking. "It's no secret that Michael Devant is one of the richest men in the county and probably the richest in Missouri."

"Yeah, it's common knowledge."

"The man has connections all the way to the White House and most of them he has dirt on and the other ones he'll find something."

"I don't understand what that has to do with me," Chase replied.

"Everything, that piece of explosive equipment you found at that explosion at Elaine's parent's house was from her father-in-law's company."

"Are you sure?"

"Trust me, I've seen and heard a lot on my way up, I know what I'm talking about."

"I was waiting in the lab to tell me where it may have come from," Chase said.

"You'll be waiting for a while. Michael's influence has no limits and that device won't make it back to you."

Chase looked shocked at what the Captain was saying, what he was hearing, but not what was being said. This is something he had always thought in the back of his mind and needed proof.

"With those connections he's managed to get approval from the chief of police to bug your friend's home and her parents home."

"For what, hasn't he destroyed her family, now what's he going after?"

"Her whole family."

"When I was a kid I used to hear about Mr. Devant and how he would manipulate people from all walks of life, I was told by my mother that she hoped to God I'd never have to work for him."

"Don't get too worked up about it, it won't do your friend any good," the Captain said, switching over from his burrito to his big, nasty, wet cigar.

"So why are you giving me the heads up this early in the game?" Chase said with a puzzled look.

"Your friend has a court date Friday to see if she is fit to be little David's mother."

"How did you know about that?"

"Have you been listening, Chase? These two families are like royalty in St. Louis, with one family representing good and the other one having the devil as the head of the household."

Clearly the Captain had no love for the man and conceivably the hate list for him was probably about as long as a football field. With this type of hate you'd have to be watching your back, even in church.

"I see you got the package," looking down at Chase's hands.

"I guess I'm not good at hiding things that well," Chase replied.

"You'll get better shortly."

"Did you send this to me, Captain?"

"Let's just say the powers that be want to make sure you find what you're looking for. Even if—"

"Even if what, what were you gonna say, Captain?"

"Never mind that, you just be careful," the Captain said, going through his desk drawers.

Chase looked down at the side of the desk and saw a box full of the Captain's belongings. "Going somewhere, Captain?"

"Yeah, early retirement."

"You'll be missed by everybody," Chase said, giving him a smile.

"From your lips to God's ears, but thank you."

The rookie Chase had scolded earlier was looking into the office, wondering what was going on. He was trained to be observant and analyze a situation quickly, but somehow this may not have been it. The young man saw Chase as someone he could look up to in the department. His eagerness to be a part of things would come in handy in ways this rookie never imagined.

"Okay, Captain, I'll see you around," he said, opening up the office door.

"Oh, and Chase."

"Yeah, Captain?"

Looking out his office window, "Do us all a favor and bring Michael Devant's ass down."

"I'll do my best."

"Hey Lieutenant, if you need anything just let me know sir."

Chase looked over his shoulder at the squeaky, not yet masculine voice shouting to him. THere was only one person in the department with that voice, the overly friendly rookie.

"Come here, rookie. What's your name?"

"Officer Williams, Jermaine Williams, actually," he said, extending his hand.

Chase looked down at his hand and shook hands with a tight grip, sizing the young man up. He looked at the rookie and saw a big smile on the rookie's face. Normally, Chase didn't trust people who smiled a lot , but he could tell this was the rookie's nature and disposition.

"Your face ever get tired?"

"I don't understand what you mean, sir," still smiling.

"You smiling all the time."

"No, sir. I like people and being a cop, I'll try my best to treat everybody fairly."

"How long have you been in full gear?" Chase asked, giving him the once over.

"A week, sir."

"Well you made it to a week already, there might be hope for you."

Laughing, "Yeah, I guess I have, sir."

"Don't you be so eager, everything will happen for you, as long as you do your job the way it's supposed to be done, all right?!"

"Gotcha."

"Isn't that right, Detective Stevenson?"

"Don't let the Lieutenant corrupt you, rookie," he replied smiling.

"I'll try not to, sir."

"Gotta go, I'll see you both later," Chase said, heading towards the elevator.

ELAINE AND HER FAMILY, with Cisco and the social worker behind them, walked into the house. They all walked into the living room, taking their respective places to sit down, as if this was an actual trial. David said hi, waving his little hand at the new stranger now in his living room. Lucile, I'm sure, was ready to throw him out on his ass, but for the sake of her family she held her peace.

"First of all, let me start by introducing myself. My name is Gabirel Carrillo and I'm–"

"I already know who you are and what you want. My question is, who sent you here and why?"

"I'm from the department–"

"Look, I don't know why my son-of-a-bitch for a father-in-law even petitioned to have full custody anyway."

"Ma'am, getting upset won't diffuse the situation or this assessment meeting," the social worker said, opening up his briefcase with enough paperwork to assess every home in the city.

"Has it ever occurred to you that maybe this isn't one of your typical home visits and that there's no problem here, or are you conditioned by your own years of experience?" Elaine said, putting her hands on her face.

The social worker looked over at Cisco and wondered if he was the boyfriend, and was he the reason this obviously good woman had to go through all this. To him , he looked a little rough, but maybe that's how she liked her men.

There were no signs of child abuse or neglect, the house was immaculate and no bad odors, not his typical home visit. Although this was a good thing, he kept in the back of his mind that he was sent here for a reason, her father-in-law notwithstanding.

"Explain to me what happened with the home catching fire a while back?"

"In a nutshell, someone tried to kill me and my son and it–"

"Wait, did you say someone's trying to kill you and your son, are you sure?"

Elaine didn't know if she should sit there and laugh or ask to see his ID to see if he was on the level, because she couldn't believe him. "Have you been watching the news, Mr. Carrillo or were you smoking dope these last couple of weeks?" She shouted across the room.

"Elaine, calm down sweetheart, you have enough on your mind, you don't need to get upset," her mother said.

"To answer your question, someone threw two molotov cocktails in my living room window, almost burning my whole house to the ground."

"Was David in the house at the time?"

"Yes, he was in his bedroom sleeping."

"When did you notice the fire?"

"I was in his bedroom checking on him because I had heard a noise and he was okay, but I saw flickering shadows on the wall and left the room to see what it was and I first smelled smoke and then saw flames. I ran back upstairs and got David," She answered, looking off in the distance.

"Was that the only occurrence that happened in these past couple of weeks, because–"

"No, there was one more."

Elaine was explaining to the social worker about the car explosion, that other occurrence. Cisco discreetly walked out of the room, looking around the house. Lucile didn't grow up on the streets, but she had enough common sense to know this man knew something she didn't. She followed his lead and discreetly left the room.

Cisco walked into the den, taking his hand underneath the surfaces of the furniture and anything else he could put his hands over. Lucile peeked in the den, watching him go through the room like some dog looking for drugs.

"Any particular thing you're looking for?" She replied, folding her arms with a stern look.

Cisco put his index finger on his lips and waved his head side to side. Lucile looked puzzled and quickly realized why he motioned her to be quiet because she'd seen something in his hand she hadn't seen before.

It was a clear, square, almost invisible chip in his hand. Lucile had only seen microphone bugs in the movies and they were round. Lucile realized at that moment her and her family were in good hands as long as he was around.

———

Chase was driving down a one-way street to the location and quickly realized he was coming up on an old, abandoned coal plant warehouse that used to be a favorite place to go for him and the few friends he had. There was a black new-model Mercedes with no plates parked at the end of the street. This was at the end of the plant, where there was a ditch there were sometimes people would dump their junk and waste into.

Carefully observing his surroundings, he parked his vehicle at the opposite end of the street in case someone wanted to try and prevent him from getting away if he needed to. He walked around to the front entrance, which was directly in front of the ditch. He wondered if anybody had ever been thrown over into it but didn't want to think about it too much at the present time.

He walked in the door and quickly was hit with complete darkness, except for a single light shining in the rear of the plant. This was one of those times he wished he had a flashlight to guide him in. He had only the moonlight to guide him through the darkness of the plant, which was beaming through the broken window up above.

Getting closer to the light, he heard what sounded like mice or rats running along, trying to get away. He looked up and saw in fact it was a mother racoon and her three babies running across the upper level stairway that was lit up by the moonlight. He started to think that he must've been out of his mind for doing something like this.

Reaching the other end where the light was, he now saw that the light was shining down on what seemed to be a small, worn card table with an envelope on it. Just as he was reaching for the envelope, out of the corner of his eye he saw a shadow of what seemed to be a person standing above. Suddenly, Chase drew his .45 and pointed directly at the figure above.

"Who the hell are you?"

"Someone who isn't a threat, but can help you and those you're trying to help piece this all together.Calm down, have you forgotten why you were sent here?" The figure above replied.

"This whole thing is getting stranger by the second," he replied, still pointing the gun at the figure.

"Put the weapon away, I'm not your enemy."

Chase slowly put his weapon away, but kept his eyes focused on the figure above and a steady hand on his weapon just in case. "So what's in the envelope?"

"I'm just here to make sure you get it."

"You one of the powers that be the Captain was talking about?" Chase asked.

"Everything you need for your part of this puzzle is in that envelope to take care of our beloved Mr. Devant," the stranger replied, closer into the moonlight.

Chase opened up the envelope and found a disc that wasn't labeled. Somehow this didn't seem strange considering everything else.

"What's on the disc?" He asked.

"Names, dates, documents, etc," the stranger replied.

"Okay, that explains the disc, but what about the key?" Chase asked, holding the key in his hand.

"To answer your first question, you'll find out soon enough, and the second one, that key you have will open up a metal box near the door you came through," the stranger said, pointing in that direction.

Chase put the envelope with the disc in it in his inside pocket of his blazer and started walking. He thought that if this was a trick, it was the most elaborate, detailed and all the cloak and dagger that comes along with it. Having no way to see anything, he relied on the moonlight coming through the broken window above.

Reaching the entrance, he opened the door and shone some light on the inside and not only saw the metal box but a light switch on the walls that he had somehow missed on his way in, but that wasn't exactly on his mind coming in. He hoped this would be his last encounter like this where he made himself vulnerable.

Curiosity got the best of him and he flipped the switches and no power came on on that end of the building. He wondered why any power was in this place, after all, it was abandoned. Maybe this stranger was adept in electrical work , he thought to himself.

The metal box was on the floor waiting to be unlocked and looked into to show the secrets it kept. Chase turned the lock and lifted the top of the box and found another key. This was an old key from hundreds of years ago. He looked back and saw that the stranger's shadow had disappeared from the moonlight and heard what seemed to be a car pull off.

He quickly ran out, holding on to his new gift and headed to the street where the unplated vehicle was at. Chase arrived on the other side, but he could see that it was already driving away. Trying to catch the vehicle, he knew, would probably be impossible, and wouldn't try. Besides, there was something more important like seeing what was on the disc and what this key opened.

Although Michael Devant was no friend of his, he wondered if he would've been so inclined to do all of this if it weren't for Elaine. People just don't go up against a man like Michael Devant, but his character and his love for his friend would make that an obstacle he was willing to cross by any means necessary.

IT WAS late and the interview with the social worker was wearing thin on Elaine's nerves. She had noticed her mother and Cisco had left the room and wondered what was going on . THis was one of the many times she'd wished Rudy was here to help her through this.

David reached in his pocket and pulled out a piece of bubble gum. "Hey stranger, you want some of my bubblegum?"

"No thanks, little guy."

"Are you here to take me and Mommy away?"

"No, I'm here to help you and your mommy so you can stay together," he replied, smiling at David.

Elaine thought to herself that he wasn't trying to take the two of them away, but definitely one of them. This was the longest interview she'd ever had and wasn't going to benefit from it. Her father-in-law had his hand in everything and everyone, the Department of Social Services was no different.

Lucile and Cisco were back in the den finding any listening devices that were planted inside the room. If there were any more they were gonna have their hands full, it was a big house. David left the room and started to walk towards the den and saw Cisco and his grandmother going over every piece of furniture in the room. To his little eyes it looked like they were playing some kind of game.

"Can I play?" David said, chewing with too much gum in his mouth.

"Shhh," his grandmother whispered softly, coming towards David, grabbing his hand and taking him out of the room.

Kneeling down at David. "David, I want you to do something special for Grandma, okay?"

"Okay," he replied, still chewing the grape gum in his mouth that had now turned his lips purple.

"Grandma wants you to be real quiet, okay?"

"Okay, but that's not a fun game, Grandma."

"Yes, honey, I know, but Grandma will take you shopping for a new toy, okay?"

"Yay!"

Cisco looked at David and smiled and wondered what it felt like to have a family who loved you. This little boy was obviously surrounded by people that did. Cisco's mother died when he was really young and was sent to his aunt's house because his drunken father would blame him for his mother's death. She died of cancer immediately following Cisco's birth. Life with his aunt was terrible and he eventually was put in a foster home.

After having gone from one foster home to the next, he eventually got of age when he could be on his own and make a life for himself. He always, as a child, liked to build things and one day got a job with a construction company and gained the knowledge to one day have his own company. This, of course, was short-lived success because of Micahel Devant.

"Ms. Lucile, can I call you Lucile?"

"Yes, you can," she replied with a smile that barely was seeable under the circumstances.

"Everybody seems to hate Michael Devant for the things he's done, anything you'd like to share?"

"Hating is wrong no matter what side you're on."

"No disrespect, but there's a good chance he may be the

cause of all this and you don't seem to be angry," he said looking at her curiously.

With her breathing suddenly speeding up, "Listen here. young man. I loved my husband deeply and we were wonderful to each other and I loved to wake up and see his young face and the old one in later years, but what good is hating going to do, especially now?"

"I'm sorry ma'am, with every–"

"Somebody has to be strong on the outside so we can make it through this, when the time is right there won't be enough tissues to hold back the tears."

"I'm sorry, I'm being selfish and not thinking truly about how this has affected all of you, I hate him so much I forget other people have suffered."

"Apology accepted."

The two of them got back to the business of looking for those unwanted bugs. Lucile never thought she'd be looking for bugs in her home, especially not these kinds. They were always a down-to-earth, humble family who always shared their wealth with those in need, but still, bad things happen to good people.

HIS EYES WERE FOCUSED on the road, trying to conceive what had just happened and what this key and disc would reveal in this crazy rollercoaster ride. If making Captain was in his future, he was getting an early start. He'd never had to fire his gun in his whole career, but somehow he knew that might change.

His cell phone rang but he decided not to answer it and didn't believe anything was more important than discovering what was on that disc and how it would help him understand all of this. Suddenly there was a terrible feeling that came over him that something was wrong. His gut feelings were always right, no matter what was going on.

———

She walked into the bedroom, stumbling, looking at what was the most disgusting and evil person anyone would ever lay their eyes on. "So who's demise are you planning, the great and almighty Michael Devant?"

"You're fucking drunk, why am I not surprised?" He replied, smoking one of his stoagies.

"All alone in a room, wow, you'd think a man like you could

at least pay somebody to keep you company," she replied, heading towards the bar for a refill.

"Who needs friends, sky, when I've got a slut wife who reminds me why I don't need anyone to talk to."

"Oh yeah, and you're so wonderful to be around, you son-of-a-bitch," She said, pouring another glass of scotch straight up, she always wanted to taste every bit.

"For the life of me, I can't figure out why I married you."

"I can, in three words, my daddy's money."

"Oh yeah, one of the best reasons to marry, I keep forgetting. I don't know who is worse, my father for literally selling his daughter to the highest bidder, or you."

"Quit being so melodramatic, you've had a better life than most. I'd be glad I'm not on the street," he said, rising up from his leather throne, as everybody called it. "You'd be doing us all a favor if you put one in your head, sweetheart."

"Not before I blow your damn brains out first, piece of shit, no good bastard," she said, raising her glass in a toast.

"You've always been an ungrateful bitch who didn't know how to shut her mouth."

"Men like you usually die alone and bitter, not really knowing what true love is about," she said, pouring more scotch into her glass, making sure everydrop came out of the bottle.

"Oh I know what it is, just not with you."

"Here we go again, your never ending and undying love for that bitch," she said, taking another sip of her three hundred dollar bottle of scotch.

"She's a better woman than you'll ever be."

"Apparently so, she didn't marry you."

Michael moved closer and with all his force he slapped her, causing her to turn and fall face down on the bar. With his other hand he grabbed her hair and dragged her off the bar and slammed her head into a wall. Her arms were swinging wildly, trying desperately to undo herself from his grip.

Remarkably, she still had the glass of scotch in her hands

with a tight grip. His grip had slightly loosened, moving her over to the fireplace. She could feel the heat coming from the flames. This was her chance to escape what would be her death for sure if she didn't act quickly.

"Bitch, you're gonna learn some respect right now."

She managed to get to her feet and focus on the poker on the side of the fireplace. Dropping the glass of scotch in her left hand, she put both hands on the poke and swung, hoping she'd hit him somewhere that would completely free her from his grip. The poker had made contact where it surely gave her the upperhand."

"You fucking bitch, you blinded me."

His grip was released and she quickly stumbled over to the other side of the room, behind the bar, bending over, searching for the knives they used often to cut lemons and limes for drinks. Her hair was in her face, almost blinding her from seeing her last option to defend herself.

"I'm gonna kill you, you stupid bitch," he shouted with his hand covering his right eye.

He could only see with his left eye, trying to move forwards towards her. With his left hand he was tossing anything in his way, trying to make good on his threats.The poker was glowing behind him by the flame with the redness of the blood glistening on it.

"Come on, motherfucker, I've been waiting for this," she shouted, coming from around the corner with the knife.

"You don't have the guts to finish it."

Sky's heart was racing and her body was full of adrenaline, waiting to strike if Michael made one wrong move, and this would be the 'til death do us part' part of the vow, she enjoyed to end this unholy matrimony. She quickly, still with the knife in her hand, put her hair in a knot and was ready to take him on.

"You come and see if you can."

Jessica, one of the servants in the house, walked in and saw what must've been a war zone to her, with both sides at a temporary ceasefire. "My God, what happened here?"

"Never mind that, call the police and have this bitch arrested," Michael shouted with blood coming out of the corner of his right eye.

"Right away Mr. Devant."

She quickly left the room and started dialing for the police. Calling the police was never done before, usually the two of them would go to their separate areas of the mansion and stay there for days. Why the two of them ever came back to the same room was beyond her.

"Jessica, stop," Sky shouted from the bedroom, "Michael, you really don't wanna call the police, I'd hate to talk to someone and be interrogated and have something slip out, darling."

"You don't know shit about what I do and how I do it, slut."

"Oh on the contrary, my devoted and loyal husband, I know quite a bit, where would you like me to start?"

"You're bluffing."

"Two words: Omega Project."

Suddenly, Michae, realized his wife had the upper hand and may know something that could ruin him and his life. She'd finally pulled her trump card and was holding firm. At that moment, his wife had truly become his enemy. Like all his enemies, silence was the key to their staying alive and she would be no different.

Disgusted with the turn of events, he ordered Jessica to put the phone down and return to what she was doing. Sky held her head high for the first time in this marriage and was proud.

THERE WAS A POUNDING in her head that seemed like it would never go away. The source of this was currently coming from this interview and everything else that seemed to make no sense at all. She focused on Rudy's face and somehow she felt the pain subsiding. This became a therapy that always had good results.

"Are there any more questions?"

"Just a few more and I'll be on my way."

Throwing him out of her home was on her mind from the jump, but really was never a reasonable option. Most people didn't realize exactly how much power a social worker had when it came to the welfare of a child.

"What role has Michael Devant played in young David's life?" He asked, pulling out a notebook.

"A destructive one, if you really want to know the truth."

"How so?"

Elaine rolled her eyes in disgust and started to wonder who this man was actually working for. "He's been trying to take my child, and our normal lives from the both of us, away."

"Maybe with everything that you stated that's been going on he felt it would be safer if his grandson was with him, is that possible?"

"Not in a million fucking years, Mr. Carrillo!" She shouted.

"Ma'am, there's no need for that, I realize this is a stressful situation for everyone involved."

"you have no idea what this situation is all about, and if you did, Michael would make sure your life was a living hell."

"Well I've asked you all the questions I have, are there any you have for me?" He said, putting away his notebook and pen.

"Yes, I'm going to need your business card, your supervisor's name, and something with your agency's letterhead on it."

He handed her a piece of paper while snapping up his briefcase. "This is a copy of Today's assessment interview."

"Sure thing, I'll file this in my file cabinet in the kitchen," she said sarcastically.

The social service worker gave her a look of uncertainty and quickly realized she more than likely meant the garbage. He grabbed the briefcase and said goodbye and was shown the door. Elain e was never so pleased to show someone the door to her home. Her father-in-law would've been the exception, but he would've never gotten in the door.

CHAPTER
TWENTY-EIGHT

THE AREA STARTED to get familiar and more thoughts of sorrow came over him. He had come up on the construction site on Chateau and Missouri Ave where Rudy had lost his life. The twelve story luxury condo building wasn't completed due to Rudy's death. Chase knew the area well, it was the Lafayette Square area, he was once doing his beat in this area of town and walked upon an older couple having a domestic squabble, and being a rookie, didn't quite know what to do.

"What;s the problem here, folks?"

"My husband's been threatening me and I want him arrested to the full extent of the law, officer," she replied on the other side of this black, shiny Rolls-Royce with license plates that read: Mr. D.

"Has he hurt you, ma'am?"

Stumbling to keep herself from falling down, "Didn't you hear what I said? He threatened me, arrest me!"

"Sir, did you threaten her?"

"Look, Rookie, can't you see she's fucking drunk."

Chase looked over at her and studied her behavior and without a doubt, she fit the profile of what he learned in the police academy, which is the profile of a typical street drunk. This obviously was a woman who had money and could have anything that she wanted, but just wasn't good at holding her liquor.

Chase Decided to write a report and log it as his first official report in his career, being the first one in his class. He'd never been so excited. Finally after three months he would get one in.

"Sir, what's your name?"

The man moved closer to Chase, bringing his head up. "You write that report and you'll find out real quick who i am, rookie."

"Goddamnit, I want him arrested," the woman shouted across the vehicle.

"Bitch, shut your cake hole or I swear right now I'll–"

"If the two of you don't settle down, I'll have to take you both in," he said with sweat rolling down his face and trembling like a crack addict going through withdrawal.

"Let me tell you something, you snot-nosed accidental fuck-baby, I'll have you fired faster that you can pull your dick out of your pants and piss on the ground, you got that?"

He'd just completed the academy training and didn't want to lose his new job. He didn't know who the man was but looking at the car, the man's suit, and all the jewelry, he figured he was important. This is one report he wouldn't log in. He had a strong feeling he'd see these two again and probably at it again in St. Louis.

The sire was abandoned with a huge fence erected around it with the skeleton of the building in the background. He parked the car on the side of the building on the Missouri Ave side. This part of the site still had a lot of trees on it and someone or something like a vehicle could easily be hidden.

Chase got out of the car and moved slowly through the brush and suddenly heard a noise. "Who's there?" He shouted, grabbing his .45

The moonlight shone through the trees like a little child playing peek-a-boo. He saw in the moonlight a little white tailed rabbit eating some greens. A smile came over his face as he put his weapon back in its holster.

Going deeper in , he noticed a clearing that led to an opening in the fence that was cut away. It was as if they cut it out especially for him. He thought the whole thing was a little weird, meeting out on this abandoned site, but nothing about this shit was exactly normal.

Chase was a few feet in front of the building when he saw a light in the distance, it was coming from the office trailer. Drawing his .45 again, he slowly moved towards the trailer. This was the first time he might be firing his gun and was more than willing to accommodate whoever might be inside.

His weapon was pointing at the door of the trailer, hoping for the best, but expecting the worst. "Who's in there?" He shouted.

No one answered and he slowly approached the door, still aiming his .45 at the door. He opened the door, slowly checking for any surprises. Nothing was on, but the desk light on the desk where there were papers scattered all over.

There was a sudden noise behind the door, Chase suddenly maneuvered himself inside the trailer, keeping his eyes and weapon firmly fixed on the door and who, or whatever, it was coming out from behind the door.

"Who's there, if you don't come out right now, I'm gonna fire my weapon."

"Don't shoot," a voice shouted behind the door.

"Then you better get your ass out of here now, with your hands in the air."

Two hands slowly came from behind the door, on the right-hand wrist there was a yellow band like the ones people wear all over the place and probably don't know what it's for.

More of the unseen body came from behind the door of the trailer. After the arms, he saw a foot, then another, and then all the family jewels came dangling out with a tattoo above them that said 'These are for the ladies' with an arrow pointing at them.

"What the hell are you doing behind their butt naked?"

"I was, you know."

Chase was puzzled by what he said for a second, and realized quickly where he was going. "If you were playing with yourself on the way out here, it's pathetic and weird."

"No, no, I'm with my girl, officer," the kid said with his barely there chest breathing fast.

"Alright, come on out, sweetheart, and for pete's sake, cover yourself up."

She slowly came from behind the door with her hands up.

"I said cover yourself up," Chase replied, shaking his head.

The young girl was shaking at the sight of his weapon, pointed right at them. She was a beautiful girl and naked. Chase couldn't get distracted, no matter how beautiful she was.

"Officer, I mean Lieutenant," she said with an innocent smile.

"You know me?"

"Sort of, my father works with you at the precinct."

Suddenly, Chase started to remember who she reminded him of and felt awkward about seeing her naked with her hands up in the air. "Are you Sgt. Morales's daughter?"

"Yeah," she replied smiling.

"The both of you, put some clothes on now!"

Chase tried not to look at her but she had grown into a beautiful, brown-eyed, voluptuous, dark-haired young Latina woman. The boyfriend, with his green eyes and curly hair, reminded him of a young Christoph St. John.

"I want to see your ID when you're done too."

"Please don't tell my father, sir–"

"–or mine!" The two of them said, nervously putting their clothes on.

The two of them showed Chase their identification and both of them turned eighteen today, this was one hell of a coincidence. He thought these might be fake, so he went into investigation mode.

There had been a lot of fake IDs being made lately and the

two of them could very well be carrying around fake ones. He'd had a feeling these were fake so he asked one question.

"What month were you born in?" he asked.

"Umm."

"'Umm', don't you know when you were born?" he asked, thinking he'd caught her up.

"August 23rd," she replied, buttoning up her last button on her shirt.

He still wasn't convinced that she wasn't lying and probably practiced saying the date over and over until she knew it by heart. The boyfriend probably had it down pat, usually they were the ones making the IDs for their girlfriends, at least that's how Chase remembered it when he was around that age.

"What about you, Romeo?"

"I was born August 23rd, 1987, sir."

He'd expected nothing less of the boyfriend, like he figured, he'd have it down. "Okay, smart ass. I'm gonna write down your names and info in case I see you again."

"We won't be a problem for you any more, I swear it."

"What are you, the brains of the operation?" Chase said to the name he'd given to the boyfriend.

"No."

"Then shut your mouth," he said, putting his weapon back in its holster.

"I'd better not ever see the two of you here anymore, and tell all your teenie bopper friends they'd better stay away too,," he said, giving them back their IDs.

The two of them started laughing like five year olds, covering their mouths.

"What's so damn funny?" He shouted.

"Sir, nobody says 'teenie bopper'"

"Well I do, and be quiet," he said, smiling back at them.

"This is a popular spot tonight."

"Excuse me?" Chase replied.

"There was a vehicle here before us, and somebody got out and went inside the office trailer," the both of them nodded.

"Did you see who it was that came in here?"

"Couldn't really see who came in, sir, but it was a man, we know for sure."

Chase started wondering who'd have any interest in coming here and ransacking the place. Well, fortunately for the two kids, they were ruled out, but he had suspicions on a few people.

"What about the vehicle?"

The two of them looked at each other and paused, like there was more to tell. There was something on the license plate, a letter or name."

"Like what?"

"I don't know, like some alphabet word or something," the boyfriend replied.

The girlfriend made a sucking sound with her lips and started shaking her head, "it was one of the letters in the alphabet, like near the front or something."

Chase couldn't believe what he was hearing out of the kids. He guessed the two of them weren't exactly honor students in highschool.

"Exactly who is your father?"

"You probably don't know my father or his family."

"Try me."

"Well, my aunt is Elaine Devant."

"What? I didn't know Elaine had a nephew."

"I'm my Daddy's little secret that he didn't tell the family about until a couple years ago," he said humping his shoulders.

The young man probably was depressed about the whole thing and why his dad did what he did. Chase didn't want to interfere and probably would eventually find out through Elaine.

"You kids get out of here and go straight home."

"Sure thing, Lieutenant."

The two of them gave him a little grin and rushed out the

office trailer and ran through the site to the fence where the opening was and disappeared. At that moment, he realized that the two kids must've cut the hole in the fence.

He put on a pair of gloves, being careful not to disturb anything that may help him. looking behind the door, he saw condoms and lubricant on the floor. He was shocked when he saw this, he figured they weren't completely dumb.

None of the papers he saw or uncovered gave him any clues, because whoever was there before the kids may have taken it. He decided to leave things as is and turn the light off and leave and get to the business of his new gift.

THERE WAS silence in the home, something that had become very strange in her life and couldn't go unchecked. She walked around from room to room until suddenly she saw her mother touching the furniture with David at the entrance to the den. The closer she got to the den, she could see Cisco kneeling on both knees, feeling and looking under the window pane.

Pulling on Elaine's pants leg, David had his little finger on his lips, "Mommy, you have to be quiet, they're looking for something," he whispered.

"What are they looking for?"

"I don't know, Mommy, but Gramma said if I'm quiet she'll buy me a toy."

"She did?"

"Yep. Tommy down the street said his Mommy's got all kinds of toys."

"For Tommy?" She asked.

"Nope, for herself."

"What?"

"He said she has a toy that she puts between her–"

"That's enough David, I'm going to have a talk with Tommy's mother."

"Why, Mommy?"

"I don't want you playing with one of her toys when you visit Tommy again, by mistake."

It was none of Elaine's business, but the things she was hearing about Tommy's mother weren't exactly breaking news, she had heard it before. This time it was from her son and that was just not a good thing. Lafayette Square was well known for its dirty secrets if you cared to ever listen to what was being said.

Lucile glanced over at Elaine and stopped searching and walked over to Elaine. "We need to be as quiet as possible, there are listening devices in the den and probably in the whole house."

"How many?"

"A few, not too many."

"Where's Victor when you need him?" Elaine replied.

"You know your brother ain't exactly one for family meetings."

"He's always been there for me, why have things changed?"

"He hates us, me and your father, maybe he felt we didn't love or support him enough."

"Did you?"

"Elaine, look, me and your father built a very successful real estate company and we worked for it, your brother had no concept of that," she replied, gently caressing Elaine's face.

"Maybe he just needed someone to believe in him."

"You became the best nurse in this state because you worked for it, why couldn't he have done the same."

"I don't know, maybe he needed more."

"More what, Elaine? He had all the money he could want because of me and his father."

"Let's hope he's made peace with himself about things that have happened in his life," Elaine replied.

"I've done all I could. I taught him right from wrong, to be good to himself and others no matter who they are, and I've loved him as much as a mother could, I'm done."

"Speaking of being done, is he done finding those things?"

"Well, I only found one and I had no idea where to look and got lucky, I'm sure he'll find a whole lot more," Lucille replied.

Cisco got up on his feet and walked towards Elaine and her family with as many listening devices in his hand as possible.

He motioned Elaine and her family to follow him out of the rear entrance near the middle of the lawn. It was a nice, sunny and breezy day in St. Louis, so it was nice to be outside, no matter what it was for.

"So, what's the verdict?"

"Not good, look at these," he said, opening up his hands, unveiling six microchips.

"How long do you think they've been there?" Elaine replied, looking down at them.

"I wanna see, I wanna see, Mommy!"

"Why are they crushed?" Lucile asked.

"I destroyed them as soon as I found them."

"Why not keep them in the house so they'll be none the wiser?" Elaine asked.

"We're obviously getting closer to finding out exactly who and what was involved with Rudy's death."

"I wanna see, Mommy," David said, jumping up and down.

David pulled down Cisco's hand. His eyes opened up like he'd seen his favorite toy in the store. "Mommy, I saw one of those in your room, Mommy, that day before the other day."

"Where, honey?"

"On the back of the dark stand," he said excitedly.

"You mean the night stand, honey?"

"Yep," he replied, shaking his head.

"How would whoever did this have had time to get in here and do this?" Lucile asked.

Elaine took a seat on the bench where she and Rudy would sit for hours laughing and sometimes saying nothing at all, but just holding on to each other. Only this time there was so much jow, only anger and frustration. Even when he's not around, Michael was ruining her life and anyone else who was in it.

"So what's our next move?" Elaine asked.

"Well, by now they've, whoever they are, have figured out we know about our little friends here," Cisco replied, looking down at his handful of listening devices.

They'd decided to search the house and find as many devices as they could. The search went on for hours and more and more bugs were found. No room had been missed, not even the bathroom, which Elaine thought might not have one, but was sadly mistaken when one was found behind the lighted mirror.

Elaine's life was like a movie-of-the-week, only she didn't know how it was going to end. One thing was for sure, she decided that there would be no more tears, frustration, and certainly no more feeling hopeless. There was a new Elaine rising from this bench, one that was ready to take down her dearly beloved father-in-law.

"This might not be the best place to stay," Cisco said.

"This is my home and we're not going anywhere."

Smiling at her, "I've never seen this side of you before," Cisco replied.

"It's about to get ugly," she replied.

"I think I like this new you, not that the old you was bad," he said with a big smile.

"Sweetheart, just be careful, I don't want to lose somebody else that I love," her mother replied.

"Whatever happens, just take care of David."

"I will but right now I have to be somewhere."

"At this time of night?"

"I'll be fine, I'm just going to see an old friend of mine, don't worry, Elaine."

CHAPTER
THIRTY

CHASE HAD LEFT the site and needed a bite to eat and decided to stop at his favorite greasy spoon, Diners' Delight, on Compton and Park. St. Louis had a lot, but this was his favorite one. He'd always get his regular plate with a pepsi. This was always collard green, cornbread, corn-on-the-cob, sweet potatoes and okra.

He was the only Japanese person to ever come inside this building, not to mention the neighborhood, but then again, he did grow up here and he always liked the food. He was always welcomed in the neighborhood by everybody who knew him. There was one girl in particular who enjoyed seeing him. She was a young, beautiful, Black girl, about twenty two, brown eyes, beautiful smile, and sun kissed skin.

"Mr. Toronaga, would you like that to-go?" She asked with a smile.

"Yes, Marnece, it's to-go, and could you make sure there's a piece of pie with that?"

"What kind?"

"Lemon pie."

"Coming right up."

"How's your mother doing, honey?"

"She's doing fine. Mrs. Johnson."

"Aren't you friends with that girl that was in the news?" she asked.

"You mean Elaine Devant?"

"Yeah, that girl. Did they ever find out who tried to burn down her house?"

"Ideas are floating," she replied.

"They're the only well-to-do people I've ever known that helped the community and not just for a spot on the five o'clock news," she said, picking up her chicken plate.

"Yes, the family has always stayed down to earth and remembered where they came from."

"I'm curious, are you and her dating, honey?"

"No, we're not," he replied with a smile.

"If you're looking for a nice young woman, I know the perfect girl."

"I didn't think that existed."

"Well, trust me honey, it does."

"Who is this perfect girl and what's her name?" He asked curiously.

"My daughter, and she's the right girl, trust me."

His own mother is always trying to hook him up with some woman. Mrs. Johnson was no different in that respect, she just didn't use a lot of tact. She did have his wellbeing in mind regardless. 'Many titles were her name', as his mother would say; Matchmaker, Peacemaker, Neighborhood Watcher, and of course, Asskicker if you tried something.

"I always enjoy hearing you talk , Mrs. Johnson. You crack me up everytime."

"Thank you, laughter is food for the soul, but to answer your question, the perfect girl is Marnece, my daughter."

"Isn't she dating someone, ma'am?"

"She will be after I give you this phone number," she replied smiling.

Chase knew Elaine could never love him the way he wanted and he did like Marnece. She was down-to-earth, pretty, and had a great smile. He decided to approach her himself, this way it would be more gentleman-like.

She had a big smile on her face. "Here you go, enjoy the pie."

"I will, and here's my number if you want to go get some coffee sometime and talk," he said with a big smile.

"That would be nice, Mr.--"

"Call me Chae."

"Okay."

Marnece started to blush as she reached for the paper with his number on it. One of the other waitresses looked on with a jealous look. A lot of the ladies liked Chase, but only one could make him smile like her. Mrs. Johnson was the exception, but she was a whole other thing.

"He's sure attractive, and those bo-legs of his is nice," Another waitress replied.

"Here you go," Chase handed Marnece six dollars to pay for the meal and dessert.

"I'll be right back with your change."

He nodded his head and headed for the door. He looked around and saw a lot of happy patrons enjoying their meals. Chase saw Marnece coming back with his change and looked over and saw a gentleman that looked familiar.

"Here you go, Chase," she said, smiling and giving him his change.

"Thank you, and call me whenever you're ready to go have that coffee," he said, smiling.

He waved goodbye to those he knew and headed out of the place with his food in hand. The streets were lit up pretty good, finally after everybody in the neighborhood got together and complained. He opened up his car door and heard a voice from across the street.

Chase looked up and over the top of the car and saw someone coming out of the shadows. Although he knew the neighborhood, there were always a few who would test you regardless. Considering what's been happening lately, nothing or no one would he given the benefit anymore.

He quickly reached for his weapon, but was careful not to draw it from its holster. A lot of good cops took the lives of young and innocent people who weren't a threat to them and were not armed. There also were the men and women who put their lives on the line everyday who never received a thank you for those that abided by the same law as civilians they tried to stop from doing the wrong thing, this was never ending.

"I'm a cop and I'm carrying so stop right there."

"I'm unarmed, I knew that was the only way I could talk to you," the voice replied from the darkness.

"Come into the street under the light where I can see you, slowly."

Slowly, the person moved out of the darkness and into the light beaming down on the dark street. He hoped he wouldn't have to shoot anyone before he had his meal, this would probably spoil his appetite.

As the light shined on the mystery person's face, Chase started recognizing the face, "Johnnie, is that you?"

"Yeah, it's me, I wanted to talk to you about something."

It was Johnnie, a guy Chase had gone to school with in junior high and highschool. He was really popular with the ladies and the fellas thought he was the mack, as they say. The two of them crossed each other's path and always greeted each other with the usual 'what's up'.

Under all that machismo, there was an intelligent guy who actually graduated from highschool. He wasn't at the top of his class or anything, but managed to squeeze in a passing grade at the end. Some say he even did all the work himself, although that's debatable considering how popular he was with the ladies and some of the smart kids who wanted to be him.

"No offense, but you mind turning around and facing away from me and holding your hands up?" Chase asked, still resting his right hand on his holster.

"Anything else you want me to do?"

"Yeah, can you slowly get on the ground with your face on the concrete?"

"Damn, am I being arrested tonight?" He said, shaking his head.

Johnnie slowly got on the ground, laying on his belly with his face facing the direction of the diner. Chase slowly walked towards him, still face-down, and started to frisk him. It wasn't uncommon for guys in this part of St. Louis to be armed like a tank. The frisking was over and he helped Johnnie up off the ground and gave him a grin.

"Wow, I never figured you would end up being a cop."

"As corny as it may sound, I wanted to make a difference in this city."

"In these streets we need more cops like you."

"So what did you want to talk to me about, Johnnie?"

"It's about Elaine Devant."

Chase was shocked that Johnnie knew Elaine and wondered what the connection was. "How do you know Elaine?"

"Growing up she was always nice to me in school and didn't make me feel dumb like a lot of people," he replied with such sincerity and compassion.

"When was the last time you spoke to her?"

"Just before she had little man David," he replied.

All this was news to Chase, he always knew Elaine was open minded about everyone and gave them the benefit of the doubt, but Johnnie was known for his escapades with the ladies and was in big trouble besides.

"She saw beneath all that overly masculine shit I was putting out there."

"That is what makes her one hell of a lady and a good friend if you ever get the honor," Chase said.

"My people on the streets say you're looking for the person or persons responsible for the fire and the murder of her father."

"Yeah, why, you got something?"

"Can we go somewhere and talk, I don't want to be seen talking to a cop right now," he replied, looking around nervously.

"Is there ever a good time for you to talk to one?"

"No, but this is someone who means something to the both of us, so maybe we can work together."

Chase was a decent , honest cop who ninety-five percent of the time always went by the book, the other five percent included fixing parking tickets, etc. Little things, nothing like this or with someone with Johnnie's street reputation.

"I don't really work with–"

"You don't really have a choice."

"Don't piss me off, okay, you can't have that much leverage," Chase replied.

"You want some leverage, how about Michael Devant, is that enough leverage?"

"Alright, where do you want to go and talk?"

"I'll let you know when we get there," Johnnie replied, opening up the passenger side of the vehicle.

"You try anything, I won't hesitate to blow your damn brains out," Chase said, looking him firmly in his face.

CHAPTER
THIRTY-ONE

LUCILE HAD DRIVEN to the one place where she knew she could get some solitude, Forest Park, This just happened to be where she had met her first love. It was a forbidden love, one that would eventually linger throughout time. In 1965 everything was political and the civil right movement was like a newborn crawling to one day get on its feet.

She was a twenty-year-old, intelligent, shy, beautiful, voluptuous, Black woman who believed good was in everyone if you helped them find it. Her mother was not as open minded and to be careful where she went, what she said, and how she said it, it was the south after all. Lucile still did what she wanted because that's who she was.

It was like any other day in the park, sunny and breezy. It was one of the few places Blacks and Whites could congregate as long as you weren't doing it together. You didn't often see two young women, one Black, one white, walking and laughing in the park together. This was something rare in the times, especially if it wasn't in protest.

The two of them would always come to the hill in Forest Park, right under the museum. They would often look out into the distance and imagine anything and everything. people would stare, both Black and White, at how they didn't have a care in the world.

The young men in the park who didn't have any girlfriends would all admire them when they went by. For Lucile, it didn't matter if the young Black men or the White men looked. Sky, on the other hand, couldn't be looked at by Black men. Although she didn't mind, there would be dire consequences for the young Black men. Even with all this love for each other and their friendship, the two of them knew what each other's reality was.

Nevertheless, Lucile and Sky did what young women did, enjoy life as much as they could, this included awning over guys. There was one in particular that Sky didn't care too much about, but Lucile thought was handsome and a gentleman. It was a young, six-foot-two, medium build, blonde haired guy with a gorgeous smile, Michael Devant.

He would always say hello to the ladies, but he always made a special effort to smile at Lucile. This was a different Michael, one who saw beauty no matter who you were, or your background. Most Black people who knew him in his younger days called him white chocolate. This was actually a term of endearment, considering what the world was like then.

As time went on, Lucile and Michael got closer and started to date. The two of them knew what this meant, that they would face obstacles from every side of this new relationship. Their families would be the most detrimental to their downfall to assure this union never survived.

Lucile had come off one of thor pleasant dates of strolling through the park and going for ice cream. "I'm home," she shouted throughout the house.

Her father came downstairs in his pajamas with a look of concern on his face. This meant two things. One, he wanted to have a 'what are you going to do for a career?' or the talk which always ended badly, 'why are you still with Michael?'.

"Lucille, I need to talk to you for a minute," he said, getting his favorite chair, his old, ratty, brown recliner.

"If it's about Michael, I'd rather go to bed and sleep."

"Talking about it later, I might not be calm," he said, giving her a look that was unmistakably serious.

Lucile took a seat on the couch in front of him and forced herself to listen. She always felt like she was on trial when she sat down with her father. Having had no college education in his life, he often wondered if he could relate with her because she was in college. Nevertheless, he always tried talking to his kids to let them know he cared.

"This relationship that you have with Michael is something you can't continue to do anymore."

She knew he had always thought the way he did but never actually heard him say it. "I'm a grown woman, I can think for myself."

"Maybe that's the problem, you're not thinking about everybody else and what we have to deal with from people outside this house."

"Daddy, I'm happy with him and I want to one day get married to Michael."

"You're living a fantasy that will never come true, trust me when I say this."

"Things are changing , Daddy, me and Michael really do care for each other."

"You're young, Lucile, you'll find someone else," he replied, getting up from his recliner.

"Does Momma agree with you on this?"

Just then, the sound of footsteps were heard coming from the hallway. It was her mother in her pink, thick house-coat with huge embroidered flowers on it in her pink slippers. Lucile would laugh sometimes when she saw her with it on. She later on discovered that she herself would be modeling this same garment and getting laughs from Elaine.

"Yes, I do honey, we want your life to be better without all the struggles and hardship that we went through," her mother replied sitting down beside her.

"But I know he loves me and wouldn't do anything to protect me from harm," she replied with tears rolling down her beautiful mahogany skin.

Lucile didn't want to face reality but knew she eventually would have to. She decided to do this on her own terms, with her and Michael alone. It killed her to even think about ever leaving him , but she knew this had to happen. This would always be a constant memory in her mind and a blow to her heart.

"Honey, you know we're just looking out for you, we know how hard this is, but you have to do it," her mother replied.

Her father sat down and put his arms around her, "I love you and this just needs to happen to protect you and him. You do wanna protect him, right?"

"Of course, I do," she answered, wiping her tears.

She rose from the chair and kissed both her parents and started up the stairs with her head down. A young lady who believed that goodness was in everybody and to always love another human being, had to destroy a human being that she loved so much.

CHAPTER
THIRTY-TWO

LUCILE WAS NOW LOOKING at the magnificent water fountain down from where so many wonderful memories were made. It was late at night and she needed to get back to get back to Elaine and David. She also knew what else she had to do for the safety of her family. Tears started rolling down her eyes as she looked down at the .38 revolver in her purse.

"Lucile," a voice called out from the darkness.

Quickly grabbing for the revolver and turning around, "Take one more step and I'll blow your brains out."

"Since when did you start carrying a pistol?"

"You get any closer, you won't have to worry about it," she replied, pointing the revolver in the direction of the voice.

There was a tall figure dressed in black coming out from the shadows into the street light. Lucile was convinced that this might be the last day she would ever see her family.

"You wouldn't hurt your son-in-law."

Just then she'd thought she'd gone crazy, "Whoever you are, I don't appreciate the sick comment. My son-in-law is dead."

"What if I told you he wasn't?"

The voice was sounding familiar, but she still couldn't take that chance. She was, after all, in a huge park that housed a lot of homeless people, unfortunately. Her purse was slipping down her arm, causing the revolver to move around. She moved back a couple of steps using her left hand to take the purse off her arm.

Hands came from the sides of this dark clothed person and slowly took off the hood that was covering the person's head. Their faces were revealed and she immediately went into shock. At that moment none of this was making sense anymore, especially what she had just witnessed. If this was a scam someone had just pulled the biggest hoax ever.

"Hello, Lucille," Rudy said with a smile.

"My God, is this really happening, am I dead?"

Rudy wanted to smile, but somehow this wasn't the appropriate time to show those pearly white. "You're not dead and this is for real."

"I don't understand, you're supposed to be dead," she said with the gun still pointed at his face,

"I can explain it to you, but first I'm gonna need you, to put the gun down."

"If you can tell me what my mother used to call me when I was younger."

"Lu Lu."

"Two easy, my favorite song."

"Superstitious by Stevie Wonder."

"Okay," she said, lowering the gun.

"Remind me never to piss you off."

"Speaking of pissing people off, your father."

"I know, none of us will have to deal with him for too much longer.:

"You know something I don't?"

"As a matter of fact, I knew too much then and too much now," he replied, waving her to follow him to the stairs of the museum.

"My death was faked, sort of."

"Don't confuse me please, I've had one hell of a shock already."

"It's no secret my father has had his hand in legal business deals to illegal ones, maybe that's why his power reached beyond normal men."

"I always heard of the alleged drug trafficking and prostitution ring in East St. Louis all the time," she said, nodding her head.

"That's not even half of it."

Lucile was shocked that all this was being confirmed, not to mention that her supposedly dead son-in-law was confirming all of it.

"Have you ever heard of the Omega project?"

"Only when I had casual conversations with real estate buyers I've worked with, the government would buy up land for the different government and corporate buildings."

"There's more, Michael, for the last twenty years has won due to him bribing, cheating, and some say, killing out the competition literally," Rudy replied.

"Rudy, your father's a powerful man, he can be persuasive when he wants to be," she said.

He didn't want to say anything but he had seen photos of Lucile and his father always hugging and kissing in them. He'd only found them when he was trying to collect family pictures for the family tree he was putting together. He couldn't help but wonder why it didn't work out.

"Is that it?" She asked.

"No, the government allocated at least a hundred million to do these construction projects, with a proviso that if you needed more and it would have to be proven to finish an extra ten million would be given per project continuously."

"So are you saying your father embezzled money?"

"That's exactly what I'm saying, I knew this just before I left and started my own company."

Lucile realized at that moment that the man she used to love had become a monster. "He used to be a good man."

"A year and a half after I started my own construction business, the FBI approached me with this information and very little evidence and they wanted me to deliver them a conviction with him confessing to numerous allegations."

"Let me guess, Michael didn't confess."

"Even better, he knew something was up and he quickly grabbed me and felt my chest and took a swing at me."

"Good Lord."

"There was one other thing that was interesting that night on the construction site."

"What was it?" She asked.

"Your son was there," he replied.

She knew Victor was isolated from everyone else, his own doing, but never dreamed he would be a part of killing someone else.

"There were enough lights for me to see it was Victor, I'm sorry you had to hear it," he said, caressing her arm.

"Do I want to know who shot you?"

He looked her straight in her eyes and didn't say a word. She knew it could mean only one thing, that it was Victor. She knew Elaine would be devastated and would probably never forgive him. Tears rolled down her eyes as she embraced Rudy tightly.

Suddenly, there were lights from a vehicle lighting up the street in front of them. The two of them quickly went to opposite sides and hid behind the podiums. The vehicle got closer and eventually stopped in front of the art museum.

"We're here," Johnnie said to Chase.

Chase was suspicious of the whole thing and really didn't understand why he was brought to the park in the middle of the night. The two of them got out of the vehicle and approached the art museum. Chase's instincts that something wasn't right was on high alert, like it hadn't been ever.

Johnnie pulled out a small flashlight from his jean pocket and flashed it twice at the glass doors in front of the building. The light shined all the way through to the fountain, showing on water flowing.

Rudy slowly came from behind the podium on his side and

took a flashlight out of his pocket and responded with three flashes. Lucile saw this and wondered who Rudy was flashing and why.

Chase stepped back and reached for his weapon. "Don't come down any more steps until you identify yourself."

Suddenly Lucile recognized the voice and slowly came from behind her side and shouted, "Please, don't shoot!"

"Come out where I can see the both of you right now."

Johnnie wanted to tell him to calm down but he was, after all, a cop and was brought to the park in the middle of the night by someone who he just met, the man was on edge and who could blame him.

"Chase, is that you?" Lucile shouted.

"Yeah, and how do you know me?"

"I'm Elaine's mother," she said, with her hands up high.

"You step down only, so I can see you," he said, moving her down the steps.

Lucile reached the bottom of the steps and moved into the light provided by the street lamp. Rudy almost wanted to laugh at his mother-in-law standing in the street at night, holding her arms up with her purse dangling from one of them.

"Mrs. Jackson, is that you?" Chase asked.

"Yes, it is honey, Elaine's mother," she shouted.

Chase moved closer and started to lower the weapon and quickly recognized her face. "Mrs. Jackson, I almost shot you!"

"That wouldn't have been good," she replied.

"No, that wouldn't have been, especially with everything going on around here."

"So what are you doing in the park at this time of night?"

"You're not going to believe this, but what if I told you that I saw someone that was supposed to be dead?" She answered with her arms still in the air.

"First thing, put your arms down. Second, I'd say you were stressed over the death of your husband and son-in-law."

Her arms were down and the purse now was on her shoulder. She looked like a deer caught in somebody's headlight. "About that, you might want to take a deep breath."

Chase figured either she was about to tell or show him something, or she started using drugs after everything and went bananas. He owed it to Elaine to give her the benefit of the doubt and listen regardless.

"There's one more person over there behind that podium at the entrance to the museum."

Rudy came from behind the podium and started down the stairs. He thought to himself he'd managed to stay alive going through all of this, it would be a shame if he actually died.

"Step into the light where I can see you."

Lucile looked over at Chase, "I hope you don't have heart problems or asthma."

"What?"

"How are you, buddy?" Rudy replied, pulling off the hood.

"Oh my God, oh my God!"

"I think he's taking it pretty well," Johnnie replied.

"I can't believe you're alive, is this some kind of hoax?"

"No, I'm alive and well, thanks to my friend Johnnie here and the FBI."

"Does Elaine know you're alive?"

"No."

"So obviously you faked your own death."

"I didn't have a choice, my father tried to kill me."

"I'd heard the man was evil, but that's just beyond evil."

"So you, Johnnie, Lucile, and myself have to send him away for life in a nice, cozy prison."

"I'm with it," Johnnie replied.

"Anyone who ever had any dealings with him, legal or otherwise, we need to find them and what they know," Rudy said.

"What about this disc, do you know anything about it?"

"First let's move out of this light and onto the steps," Rudy said, leading them to a safer spot.

"There's actually two of them, the one you have and another in a safe place."

"Am I going to see what's on it or what?"

"All of this is just so crazy. I'm waiting for pigs to start flying next," Lucile said.

"Curiosity is getting the best of me, how do you and Johnnie know each other?" Chase asked.

"The construction site where I had supposedly died was Johnnie's territory."

"I don't get it."

"I'm like an Urban Street Mogul, so to speak, he was coming in my area and we discussed some things, the rest is history."

"He said he wouldn't sabotage my efforts to build something there as long as it would benefit the community, i.e. jobs and a community center filled with computers for the people."

"So you had no idea he might be a criminal."

"All I knew was that he obviously had some deep connection to the neighborhood and we both wanted to do something for the community to let them know people cared."

"Let's get back to the disco, what's on it and how can it help us?" Lucile asked.

"Hold on."

Rudy walked over to the bushes, kneeling down, and started digging in the dirt for about five seconds when he pulled out a silver square case from underneath the ground. The three of them looked on as he pulled the square case up and dusted it off and brought it to them.

"I'm going to need that CD you have."

Chase went back to the car to get the CD and the key. He figured the key must also be a part of the puzzle as well.

"I'm dying to see what's on the CD, here you go."

He handed the disc to Rudy and was watchful as a young kid waiting for his first toy to be opened. Rudy popped open the case which happened to be a portable CD player. Now they all would see exactly what was going to bring the mighty Michael Devant down.

The screen came up and it displayed the name 'The Omega Files'. Chase realized at that very second that this was bigger than anything he'd ever come across in his career.

"This first file is of all the names of people who were involved with issuing illegal permits to my father in exchange for favors. Some of them were forced to do it, my father had dirt on them," Rudy replied, shaking his head.

"My Lord, did I see alderman Williams on that list?"

"Yes, she's on here too, Mrs. Jackson."

"She's always been a good community leader, I never thought she would've been tied up with someone like Michale," she said.

"What are those numbers next to their names?" Chase asked.

"The amount of the bribe."

"Yo, you mean to tell me the man was that cocky, he had the nerve to put this on a computer?"

"Nothing hard to believe when it's my father."

"How did you get this information? I'm curious," Chase replied, in cop mode.

"I knew something was fishy while I was working for my father, so I started to check things out."

"I'm wondering why you started to look at things and tried to sneak around?"

"Excuse me, Lieutenant."

"You rich people are supposed to stick together, especially the Devants."

"Chase, don't–"

"It's ok, Lucile, I'm nothing like that monster. I've spent the better part of my life trying not to be like him and I think I've done well."

"You have, and I'll be the first to say it," Lucile said.

"I'm sorry, I've just always been told that Michael and his family were all around evil."

"I could've easily ended up like him."

"But you didn't, and that's what counts," Johnnie said, blinking his eyes.

"What about the key?"

"Well Lieutenant, that key will open up a cctv box under the trailer you were at tonight."

With a surprised look, "You were watching me?"

"I had to make sure you weren't working for my father."

"How do you know I'm not?"

"You would've already told him about the stranger you met in the warehouse and the gifts you got," Rudy replied.

Chase knew he was right , a snitch wouldn't have hesitated to run and tell so he could look good and keep whatever favors going.

"Be glad you weren't, I had a little surprise for you in my purse," Lucile said, tapping her purse.

"Mace, ma'am?"

"No honey, this .38 revolver in here," she replied grinning.

The four of them laughed for a second or two and got back to the business at hand.

The four of them continued to look at the many files Michael had kept on people who he ever dealt with. They all were shocked at the names they recognized as well as the amounts of money linked to their names.

There was a ringing sound coming from the inside of Chase's pocket. He reached inside and pulled out his cellphone and took a call, stepping away from everyone and taking the call.

"Hello?"

"Lieu, it's me, the new rookie."

Chase was shocked and a little curious, the young kid had his personal number and was calling at this hour. "What is it?"

"I've got some news, I was trying to reach you earlier but no one answered."

"This isn't a good time, rookie, I'm–"

"The Captain's dead, sir."

"Who put you up to this, goddamnit?" He shouted through the phone.

"No one sir, the call came in a couple of hours ago."

"Who called it in?"

"His wife, they say, was coming from the basement doing laundry when she heard shots and dropped everything and ran up the stairs to find out he had been shot."

"Where did she find him?"

"On the living room couch, bleeding to death."

"Did she say if she saw who did it?"

"No, but she said she heard a car driving off," the rookie replied.

"That's it, just a car? That's one hell of a lead."

"The neighbor across the street said she saw the make and model of the car and the license plate."

"So what was it?"

"She says it was a 1965 green Jaguar with the words "Mr. D" on the plates."

Chase quickly remembered that the kids earlier tonight had told them that they had seen a car pull off from the construction site with a letter on the plate. If this was the same vehicle, there was something there he thought he was missing.

"Thanks, rookie, you did good."

"No problem, sir, and thanks."

Chase walked over to the three of them as if he'd been told the worst news of his life, "The Captain's dead, his wife found him bleeding to death on the couch."

"My God, who else is going to die in all this?" Lucile said.

"Do they know who did it?" Rudy asked, knowing already what the answer might be.

"The neighbor said she saw a 1965 green Jaguar with the license "Mr. D" on the plates."

"Those are my father's plates, I'd know them anywhere."

"You think he'd kill the Captain of the force?"

"He had to eliminate any loose ends, and the Captain was a major one." Chase said, sighing.

"He's getting desperate, I know exactly where he's headed," Rudy replied, closing the lid on the CD player.

THE THREE OF them were now inside this house, trying to have a decent night without the worries of everything that's happened. Cisco was playing checkers with David and was losing every turn or was trying to make him feel good. It had been a long time since she made a man in the house besides David, she felt safe. As attractive as he was, she wasn't ready to let her heart feel anything for anyone.

Elaine took the long trip up the stairs to the attic where David would love to play and where all the junk over the years was being collected. She kneeled down and saw it again, something that she hadn't bothered to look at in weeks. This was too much for her then, but now she was ready to revisit those memories and enjoy them. She closed the attic door and headed to the den and sat at the computer.

"Are you alright?" Cisco asked, giving her a warm smile.

"I'm fine, I was just going to inspect this disc I found in the attic."

"I'll leave and give you some time alone."

"Thank you."

"No problem."

She went ahead and put the CD in and there was a video starting to play when she heard the doorbell ring. Not expecting anyone to show up and definitely not at eleven o'clock at night, she was puzzled as to who it might be.

Elaine's anticipation was building as she reached the bottom of the stairs and went to the door and looked through the security hole. After seeing who was on the other side of the door, she almost wished she had a butcher's knife.

"What the hell do you want?" She shouted through the door.

"I just wanted to talk to you, please, I'm not here to cause trouble, Elaine."

She opened the door, only giving her unwelcome visitor very little space to see in or bum rush. Not that she would've had a problem with them.

"Please Elaine, I need to talk to you."

"Come in, you've got five minutes, Sky," She said, opening up the door, giving her a deathly look.

Sky slowly crept into the house, looking at the inside of a house she'd only seen twice in her life. "This is a beautiful home."

Elaine could hardly believe it, the ice queen was giving her a compliment. Maybe the world has finally come to an end.

"You've got four minutes, let's move this conversation to the den."

The two of them walked towards the den with Elaine in the back of Sky. Elaine could see she was a nervous wreck and started to go for a cigarette.

"I keep forgetting you don't allow smoke in this house," Sky said, putting the cigarette away in her this-season's Louis Vuitton bag.

"When are you going to say what you have to say and leave?"

"Alright, I believe Michael has been embezzling money from the government and maybe killed Rudy."

"Is this another one of your tricks?"

"No I'm not, the only person doing tricks around here is

Michael, trying to convince everyone he's so powerful and can't be touched."

"You've just been given another five minutes."

"I didn't know my son the way you did, or your parents, but he was a strong, intelligent man, especially dealing with the two of us as parents, he had to be."

"I don"t know if I should be glad you're telling me this or wondering why you're telling me," Elaine said.

"My son was a strong, business-minded person who believed in protecting the people he loved around him and the things that he created with pride."

"So what are you getting at?"

"It was no secret that Rudy and Michael despised each other and he knew his father would do anything to destroy anything that represented his son's successful triumphs."

"Sky, this isn't the time for riddles, I need to know exactly what you're saying."

"There were cameras everywhere on that construction site the night Rudy died, I'd bet my life he probably recorded who killed him that night."

Elaine was so taken back by all this that tears started to roll down her face. She didn't know a lot about the sites themselves, but knew Rudy kept some record of everything that went on in his business.

Cisco and David came in looking at the two of them on opposite sides of the room, "Elaine, what's wrong, are you alright?"

David looked over at Sky and waved hello, "Hi."

"I'm fine."

"Has your mother ever really told you about Michael?"

"No, why would she?"

"Maybe because the two of them were a couple, before you were born, but nonetheless, they were."

"How do you know this?" Elaine asked, wiping away her tears,

"Your mother and I used to be really good friends."

"Not in your life."

"I was there when she met Michael, I didn't like him but your mother adored him and he, her."

"None of this shit is true, you're a lying bitch trying to mess with my head," she said, breathing heavily.

"Elaine, I'm not lying to you, it's the truth."

"Why wouldn't she tell me, I'm her daughter?"

"Simple, she moved on and fell in love with your father and made sure they gave you and Victor a decent life, which is more that I can say for myself and Michael."

Sky walked towards Elaine, looking at the computer screen behind her playing a video. Elaine turned around to see what had her mother-in-law's attention. The three of them looked on and were horrified at what they saw. Elaine's brother, shooting Rudy in the chest twice, while Michael was beside him looking on.

Rudy had managed to creep away after getting to the edge of the floor level, but he plunged to his death. Michael and Victor quickly went to see if he in fact plunged to his death. Once they were satisfied, the two of them left and out of sight on the camera.

Elaine grabbed the phone with the intention of calling the police after what she just saw but quickly realized there would be no contact with anyone outside of the house. A thousand things ran through her mind, not one of them was good.

"Elain, what's wrong?"Cisco asked.

"The phone isn't working," she replied, looking over at Cisco.

He came over and he started playing with the phone to see if he could do any better, "I'm getting nothing, maybe something else is going on."

"Like, what?"

Within seconds, the lights went off all over the house and terrified David and the ladies. Cisco went into the defensive mode, knowing that something terrible was coming next.

"Elaine, get David upstairs now. I suggest you go too, Mrs. Devant, and grab the disc."

Frantically trying to get the disc out, "I can't get the disc out!"

"Dammnit, we're gonna forget it for now. We'll come back for it later!" Cisco shouted.

The four of them rushed up the stairs, knowing every step might be their last. No matter what happened, Elaine promised herself she would protect David by any means necessary. Sky had never moved so fast since her and Lucile were on the track team. Cisco was bringing up the rear, wondering what was going to happen to the three of them and himself.

"We need to hide David somewhere so he'll be alright," Sky said, breathing heavily.

"The two of you stay with David, I'll go and see who's in the house," Cisco said.

"You can't go by yourself, who's going to watch your back?"

Giving David a hug and a kiss, "Mommy loves you, okay?"

"I love you too, Mommy," he said, hugging her as tight as he could.

"Do something good tonight and protect my child, your grandson."

"I will," she said, with tears rolling down her face.

"Get him out of here."

Sky took David out the end of the hall for someplace for her and David to hide and ended up going into the attic. David knew something was happening, but luckily for everyone, he really didn't know what.

Elaine followed Cisco down the hall, but suddenly stopped at one of the closets in the hall. She opened the door and pulled out two steel bats Rudy played with when he would play with some of the kids at the youth center. Elaine never had a use for them until now.

Cisco grabbed one of the bats and winked at her. "Are you ready?"

"Let's do it."

The front door busted open and immediately their hearts started racing again. They reached the end of the hall and waited to see if the outside light would cast a shadow on whoever might be there at the door.

Cisco went first, slowly creeping around the wall, holding on tight to the bat and started down the steps. Elaine was close behind when she heard another crashing sound, but this time it was in the back of the house. Could there be someone else in here, or was she just imagining it?

She'd almost forgotten her brother would often sneak in the back through the kitchen when he wanted to raid the fridge. This time he was coming for something else. The one person she thought had her back was willing to shoot her in it.

They reached the bottom of the steps and saw the door opened wide and projected a view of the moon high in the sky, with an earthly view of a lonely street with one of the street lights trying to lighten the way.

Another sound from the kitchen made the two of them turn their heads and out of the darkness fire was seen and Cisco had been hit and fell to the floor. Then appeared her father-in-law out of the darkness like the devil he is.

Victor creeped in from the kitchen with the light coming through the door shining on his face, "Well, well, my beloved sister."

"You evil son-of-a-bitch, you'll pay for this if it's the last thing I do," she said.

"You always were dramatic, even as a kid, maybe that's why you were their favorite. You knew how to play with their heads," Victor said, grabbing her neck.

"What happened to you, Victor?"

"What happened to me, I got tired of playing second fiddle to you and your damn son."

"They loved you, Victor."

"Not as much as they loved you and David, me and my kid didn't stand a chance in this family."

"Rudy was good to you, you know that," she said, almost choking.

"Rudy was a big pussy who didn't have what it takes to be in a family where there was unlimited power like Michael gave me. Who do you think almost burnt down your house?"

"Victor, David could have died!"

"You think I give a fuck? No!" Strengthening his hold on Elaine.

Cisco slowly was getting on his feet, holding onto his side where blood had started to come out like a fountain. Elaine was still holding on to the bat but the more Victor squeezed, the less strength she had to hold it.

"Where's the CD?!" Michael asked, now pointing the gun directly at Cisco's already wounded body.

Suddenly something Elaine had dreaded was becoming her biggest fear, hearing the little footsteps coming down the upstairs hall. She thought only of her son seeing his mother die at the hands of his uncle.

"Momm, are you okay?!"

Michael turned his head and saw David at the top of the stairs, "You watch her, I'll get the kid, maybe she'll talk then."

Sky was directly behind him, knowing she could never forgive herself if something had happened to him. He didn't deserve to be in the middle of all this. Michael reached the top and grabbed David like he was nothing more than a bag of garbage.

"You let him go!"

Michael turned around with a tight grip on David and saw something he probably only had nightmares about, his wife pointing a gun directly at him.

With a wounded body, Cisco lunged into Victor, causing him to hit the floor and release the choke hold on ELaine. With no time to waste, she struggled up the stairs, gasping for air with one goal in mind, to save her son.

"Or what, you drunk bitch?"

"I'm not drunk today, my beloved husband."

"You don't have the guts, you slut," he said, now with his hands digging into David's little shoulder.

David looked down at the steps and saw his mother reaching out to him. Michael looked down, saw her reaching for David, and started playing tug-o-war with David.

"Michael!" Sky shouted.

He turned his head, he looked her straight in her face and she fired a shot in the head and he quickly collapsed, hitting the floor like a ton of bricks. Elaine let out a scream, thinking the worst must have happened, with David being shot by mistake. Sky, overwhelmed by the shock of seeing Michael dead, stood still, slowly releasing the gun onto the floor.

There were police and EMTs being heard in the background. Finally, Elaine thought, someone was coming to free them of this horrible nightmare. She'd spoken too soon. She didn't see or hear Cisco or Michael until she turned her head, and there was Victor, standing just beneath her with blood dripping off the side of his face looking down at her.

There was a creeping sound, suddenly a bat was coming from the side of his head, causing blood to splatter before he lunged over the step rail, hitting the floor. Cisco had barely enough strength to reach the two of them at the top, but he managed a lot tonight for a wounded man.

Quickly after, there was a flood of lights coming on outside, shining inside the house like a disco club. Elaine looked down the steps and saw figures at the door, this time she felt no evil, only goodness. it was her dead husband who had come to save her. She thought she clearly lost her mind.

"Elaine, baby, I'm here!"

"Rudy, is that you? Tell me I'm not dreaming!"

"You're not, it's me, baby," he replied, looking at the two most important people in his life.

Sky slowly came to the top of the stairs, looking down at her dead husband. She did exactly what she said she would do, she just didn't know it would happen this soon. Rudy looked at his mother standing over his dead father, knowing at that very moment she'd done something that one day she would one day be forced to do.

Rudy started to climb the stairs when he noticed a body at the end of the steps. It was Cisco, his old friend, who he always knew he could count on and this was no different.

"Hold on, my friend."

Cisco looked up, barely opening his eyes. He saw this face , one that he thought he would never, ever see like this again, "Dios Mio."

Chase rushed in with his pistol, hoping the worst hadn't happened. He saw a body face down on the floor. It wasn't Elaine, but the closer he got, his fears had not come true. He instantly looked up at the top of the stairs, it was Elaine and David and it seemed like they were alive.

"They're fine," Rudy said.

Chase looked down at Rudy and saw Cisco bleeding and grasping for his life on the steps. He quickly went to the door and shouted for the EMTs to move in. Looking back inside, he saw Mrs. Devant shaking terribly while standing over a body. Not knowing who it was, he needed her to step away from it.

Drawing his weapon up to the second floor level, "Mrs. Devant, I need you to step away from the body."

"I had to shoot him , he was going to kill us all, he was going to kill us!" She shouted through the house.

"I understand, but you've got to step away so we can help you," he said, hoping he wouldn't have to fire at her.

She slowly stepped back and leaned over onto the wall and slowly went to the floor. Chase had a sigh of relief when she hit the floor.

Rudy was at the top of the stairs now, looking at his beautiful wife and kid after all this time.

"Elaine, baby, where are you?" Lucile shouted.

"I'm up here, me and David are alright!"

"Thank God," she replied.

The EMTs rushed in with only the outside light to guide them in and to Cisco bleeding on the bottom steps. The other officers rushed in through the kitchen, up the stairs and found Sky shaking frantically while securing the area. Lucile saw Sky on the top of the stairs and what she recognized as a body a few feet from her, she could suspect it was Michael.

"He's dead!" An officer shouted.

"Who is it?" Chase asked.

"It's Michael!" Elaine shouted.

Lucile walked further in and saw another body, it was her son's, Victor, dead body lying on his stomach with his head in a pool of blood. She'd wondered why he would do such a thing but realized Victor was like a volcano, give it enough time and it would eventually explode with his jealousy as fuel.